INCORPORATION AND BUSINESS GUIDE
FOR BRITISH COLUMBIA

INCORPORATION AND BUSINESS GUIDE FOR BRITISH COLUMBIA

How to form your own corporation

J.D. James, M.B.A., LL.B.

Self-Counsel Press
(a division of)
International Self-Counsel Press Ltd.
Canada U.S.A.

Printed in Canada

First edition: April 1971
Tenth edition: November 1983
Fifteenth edition: August 1990
Sixteenth edition: May 1991; Reprinted: March 1992
Seventeenth edition: January 1993; Reprinted: August 1993
Eighteenth edition: April 1994
Nineteenth edition: January 1995; Reprinted: August 1995; June 1996; April 1997

Canadian Cataloguing in Publication Data

James, J.D. (Jack Douglas), 1943-
    Incorporation and business guide for British Columbia

    (Self-counsel legal series)
    ISBN 0-88908-783-0
1. Incorporation — British Columbia — Popular works. 2. Private companies — British Columbia — Popular works. I. Title. II. Series.
KEB316.Z82J35 1995 346.711'06622 C94-910908-8
KF1420.Z9J35   1995

Self-Counsel Press
(a division of)
International Self-Counsel Press Ltd.
Head and Editorial office
1481 Charlotte Road
North Vancouver, British Columbia   V7J lHl

U.S. Address
1704 N. State Street
Bellingham, Washington   98225

CONTENTS

TABLES

SAMPLES

AVAILABLE FROM THE PUBLISHER

In order to incorporate your company, you will need to file certain forms. You may type these yourself, but it is easier and quicker to use pre-printed forms, or, if you wish, you can take advantage of our typing service and have all the forms typed out for you. We now have software available, too. Please see the software section below for full details.

Our *Incorporation Forms* kit contains copies of the forms you will need for a simple incorporation, including the memorandum, the articles, share certificates, notice of offices, and consent resolutions of subscribers and first directors. This kit is available for $14.95 where you bought this book or you may use the order form on the next page.

The **typing service** offered by the publisher covers the cost of the pre-printed forms and the typing out of these forms according to information that you provide. We do not file the documents for you, nor does the typing service fee cover your filing fees. This service is available for $125 by calling our toll-free number 1-800-663-3007. Please read this book carefully before you call. If you have decided to incorporate a small, non-distributing company, here's how we can help you.

1. When you call, we will take your name and address and mail incorporation data sheets out to you for you to complete.

2. You reserve the name you have chosen with the Registrar of Companies.

3. You return the completed data sheets to us along with your cheque for $125. We will then type all the documents and return them to you for filing with the Registrar of Companies. Please note that, while your documents will be completed by competent personnel, we cannot and do not give legal advice. If you have complicated tax or legal problems with incorporation, you should see a lawyer.

NOW AVAILABLE — INCORPORATION SOFTWARE

Our *Incorporation Self-Ware* enables you to incorporate a company right on your own PC — $35.00 (see order form on the next page).

Features

- Stand-alone software, no word processing package is required
- Easy to install
- Menu driven
- Built-in error checking helps ensure papers are complete
- Pop-up help screens provide definitions of legal terms and explanations of important concepts
- Mouse or keyboard driven
- Free technical support available to all registered owners

System Requirements

- IBM/Tandy/100% compatible computer
- 512K RAM free
- Floppy and hard disk drives
- DOS 3.3 or higher
- Supports any standard printer

This software is intended for use on a single computer, by a single user only.

Send to: **Self-Counsel Press**
1481 Charlotte Road
North Vancouver, B.C. V7J 1H1
Fax: (604) 986-3947

✂ – *(Clip and mail)*

Please send the following items prepaid:

Item	Quantity	Unit Price	Total
Company Act	_____	$11.00	_____
*Incorporation Forms for B.C. (Kit)	_____	$14.95	_____
*Incorporation Software	_____	$35.00	_____
*Minute book	_____	$17.95	_____
*Extra share certificates	_____	.50¢ each	_____

SEALS AND STAMPS

Seals and stamps are not shipped from Self-Counsel Press. They are shipped directly from the manufacturer.

*Seal, up to 39 characters	_____	$35.00	_____
*Seal, 40 or more characters	_____	$40.00	_____
*Deposit stamp (with 2 lines)	_____	$14.25	_____
*Endorsement stamp	_____	$10.50	_____
*Name and address stamp (with 3 lines)	_____	$16.95	_____
Subtotal			_____
***Add Provincial Sales Tax to items marked with asterisk**			_____
Postage & handling books, kits, etc. (includes GST)		$3.00	_____
Postage & handling seals & stamps (includes GST)		$3.00	_____
Add 7% GST calculated on Subtotal			_____
TOTAL amount to be forwarded by money order.			_____

Or, if you prefer, you can charge your order to your MasterCard or Visa. Please fill in number, expiry date, and validation date (if MasterCard) on the form below.

All prices subject to change without notice.

(Please print)

Please send the items checked above to:

Mr./Ms._____

Address:_____

City:_____

Province: _____ Postal code:_____ Telephone:_____

Name of corporation:_____

Corporation address (for stamp) if not same as above:_____

Please charge to my ☐ Visa ☐ MasterCard

MasterCard/Visa number: _____

Expiry date:_____ Validation date:_____

Signature: _____

Please check your seals and stamps upon receipt.
We will not be responsible for errors reported more than 30 days after mailing.

Incorporation Software: To ensure you have all the relevant information to incorporate your company, you must use this form to place your order. We are unable to fill software orders unless this form is used.

SCP-INCBC 19/95

PREFACE

Why are you interested in incorporating? Probably because of your accountant's suggestion or because you have heard vague references from your friends and business associates about the advantages of having a company or maybe because you just think it's the thing to do.

Whatever your reason, you are probably confused and perhaps even frustrated at the idea of having to spend hundreds of dollars for something you know nothing about, especially when you are having trouble seeing the benefits that are supposed to accrue to you.

If so, this book is for you. For a relatively small investment, this publication will clear away those uncertainties and explain in simple, layperson's language the whys and wherefores of incorporating and, in addition, may save you hundreds of dollars in lawyer's fees.

However, there are some areas where this book cannot replace your lawyer or accountant. Specifically, if you are setting up a business where there are opposing interests, or if you are involved in intricate and complex debt or share issues, it is essential that proper counsel be retained.

If you are not involved in such a situation and you choose to do your own incorporation, by following the procedures set out in this manual, you will save a substantial amount ($100 to $600) in legal fees for incorporating a company.

In any event, if the business is successful, whether you seek competent professional help prior to incorporation or not, you will undoubtedly require the services of a qualified accountant following incorporation. Doing the books yourself is both dangerous and, in the long run, expensive.

This publication is not meant to circumvent or to derogate from the value of professional help. It is meant as an aid to persons who desire a simple incorporation and find that the money spent for professional fees may be better spent elsewhere, or for those who simply want to become acquainted with the legal and practical implications of a limited company.

— *Editors,*
Self-Counsel Press

NOTICE TO READERS

1

INTRODUCTION TO THE INCORPORATED BUSINESS

You are probably engaged in a small business or are thinking about starting one, either by yourself or with someone else. One of the first decisions you will have to make is what kind of business "vehicle" you should choose. In Canada, there are only three ways to carry on any business: through a sole proprietorship, a partnership, or a limited company. These encompass every type of business, from the smallest corner grocery store to General Motors of Canada Limited.

If you are already carrying on business and are not incorporated, you must be operating either as a sole proprietor or as a partner in a business. There are also special entities such as organizations engaged in charitable or semi-charitable enterprises, but these do not concern us here and will not be discussed. For information on incorporating a non-profit organization, see *Forming and Managing a Non-Profit Organization in Canada*, another title in the Self-Counsel Series.

a. THE SOLE PROPRIETORSHIP AND THE PARTNERSHIP

The simplest and most inexpensive legal form of carrying on any business is by registering a proprietorship (where only one person is involved), or a partnership (where two or more people are involved).

Sole proprietorships and partnerships are required to be registered in Victoria, but the cost is modest and the procedure is simple. All you need to do is select a name that is unique and cannot be confused with that of another business operating in your area and write to the Registrar of Companies in

Victoria to reserve your name. Be sure to include the appropriate fee. The Registrar will conduct a name search and send you a one-page Declaration form to fill out. For current fees, contact the Registrar of Companies at 387-7848.

In addition, sole proprietorships indicating a number of names to denote a partnership are also required to be registered under the Partnership Act. (See Sample #1 for a Declaration of Sole Proprietorship and Sample #2 for a Declaration of Partnership.)

Aside from the simplicity, the major advantage of a proprietorship or partnership is that, if you expect your business to incur losses for some time and you continue to hold down another job, you can offset all the losses in the business against your employment income. This is particularly advantageous in a husband/wife business where both spouses have outside sources of income.

However, there are some drawbacks to a partnership or a proprietorship. First, if you are involved in a partnership, you have the cost of a partnership agreement. This agreement regulates the conduct of the partners. Without it, you leave yourself wide open to problems down the road. The cost of a properly prepared agreement can be $300 or more.

Second, a proprietorship or partnership is not recognized in law as a separate legal entity. Therefore, all debts and liabilities incurred by the business become the personal responsibility of the proprietor or the partners. This means that all your personal assets are at risk, including your house and personal savings.

SAMPLE #1
DECLARATION OF SOLE PROPRIETORSHIP

Province of British Columbia

Registrar of Companies

Ministry of Consumer and Corporate Affairs

RETURN **BOTH** COPIES TO:
CORPORATE AND CENTRAL REGISTRY
940 BLANSHARD STREET
VICTORIA, B.C.   V8W 3E6

DECLARATION FOR PARTNERSHIP AND BUSINESS NAME

PLEASE TYPE OR PRINT **CLEARLY**. SEE REVERSE FOR INSTRUCTIONS AND GENERAL INFORMATION.

REGISTRATION OF: (CHECK WHICHEVER IS APPLICABLE)

☒ SOLE PROPRIETORSHIP   ☐ LIMITED PARTNERSHIP   ☐ CHANGE OF BUSINESS NAME   ☐ CHANGE IN NATURE OF BUSINESS

☐ GENERAL PARTNERSHIP   ☐ EXTRA-PROVINCIAL PARTNERSHIP   ☐ CHANGE IN MEMBERSHIP OR OWNERSHIP   ☐ DISSOLUTION DATE _____ YR / MO. / DAY

A. THIS SECTION MUST BE COMPLETED BY ALL	DEPT. USE ONLY

BUSINESS OR PARTNERSHIP NAME
Green and Company Office Supplies

MAILING ADDRESS	CITY
456 Any Street	Vancouver

DEPT. USE ONLY — REGISTRATION NO.

PROVINCE	POSTAL CODE	TELEPHONE
British Columbia	Z1P 0G0	444-5555

BUSINESS ADDRESS IN B.C. (NOT P.O. BOX)	CITY
456 Any Street	Vancouver

PROVINCE	POSTAL CODE	DATE OF ESTABLISHING BUSINESS IN B.C.
British Columbia	Z1P 0G0	YR 9 MO. 01 DAY 15

NATURE OF BUSINESS

Office Supplier

B. GENERAL PARTNERSHIP **ONLY**

NAME (IN FULL)

RESIDENTIAL OR REGISTERED ADDRESS (NOT P.O. BOX)

CITY	PROVINCE	POSTAL CODE

NAME (IN FULL)

RESIDENTIAL OR REGISTERED ADDRESS (NOT P.O. BOX)

CITY	PROVINCE	POSTAL CODE

DATE OF REGISTRATION

NAME (IN FULL)

RESIDENTIAL OR REGISTERED ADDRESS (NOT P.O. BOX)

CITY	PROVINCE	POSTAL CODE

NAME (IN FULL)

RESIDENTIAL OR REGISTERED ADDRESS (NOT P.O. BOX)

CITY	PROVINCE	POSTAL CODE

IF ANY PARTNER IS A CORPORATION, STATE PRINCIPAL PLACE OF BUSINESS IN B.C. (ADDRESS)

SIGNATURE OF PARTNER

SIGNATURE OF PARTNER

SIGNATURE OF PARTNER

SIGNATURE OF PARTNER

CERTIFICATION
I HEREBY CERTIFY THAT THE PERSONS NAMED IN THIS DECLARATION ARE THE ONLY MEMBERS OF THE PARTNERSHIP.

C. PROPRIETORSHIP **ONLY**

NAME (IN FULL)
John Joe Doe

RESIDENTIAL OR REGISTERED ADDRESS (NOT P.O. BOX)
555 Yang Street

CITY	PROVINCE	POSTAL CODE
Vancouver	B.C.	Z1P 0G0

IF A CORPORATION, STATE PRINCIPAL PLACE OF BUSINESS IN B.C. (ADDRESS)

SIGNATURE OF PROPRIETOR
John Joe Doe

CERTIFICATION. I HEREBY CERTIFY THAT NO OTHER PERSON IS ASSOCIATED WITH ME IN THIS PROPRIETORSHIP.

D. LIMITED PARTNERSHIP ONLY

ADDRESS OF REGISTERED OFFICE IN B.C.

CITY	PROVINCE	POSTAL CODE

JURISDICTION WHERE LIMITED PARTNERSHIP FORMED

IF LIMITED PARTNERSHIP FORMED OUT OF B.C., STATE NAME AND ADDRESS OF GENERAL PARTNER(S)

SIGNATURE

RELATIONSHIP TO LIMITED PARTNERSHIP

CERTIFICATION
I HEREBY CERTIFY THAT THE PERSONS ON THE ATTACHED CERTIFICATE ARE THE ONLY MEMBERS OF THE LIMITED PARTNERSHIP.

RC 101-63

SAMPLE #2
DECLARATION OF PARTNERSHIP

 Province of British Columbia

Registrar of Companies

Ministry of Consumer and Corporate Affairs

RETURN BOTH COPIES TO:
CORPORATE AND CENTRAL REGISTRY
940 BLANSHARD STREET
VICTORIA, B.C.   V8W 3E6

DECLARATION FOR PARTNERSHIP AND BUSINESS NAME

PLEASE TYPE OR PRINT **CLEARLY.** SEE REVERSE FOR INSTRUCTIONS AND GENERAL INFORMATION.

REGISTRATION OF: (CHECK WHICHEVER IS APPLICABLE)

☐ SOLE PROPRIETORSHIP ☐ LIMITED PARTNERSHIP ☐ CHANGE OF BUSINESS NAME ☐ CHANGE IN NATURE OF BUSINESS
☒ GENERAL PARTNERSHIP ☐ EXTRA-PROVINCIAL PARTNERSHIP ☐ CHANGE IN MEMBERSHIP OR OWNERSHIP ☐ DISSOLUTION DATE _____ YR / MO. / DAY

A. THIS SECTION MUST BE COMPLETED BY ALL	DEPT. USE ONLY

BUSINESS OR PARTNERSHIP NAME
J & J Groceries

MAILING ADDRESS
123 Any Street   CITY **North Vancouver**

PROVINCE **British Columbia**   POSTAL CODE **Z1P 0G0**   **222-1111**

REGISTRATION NO.

BUSINESS ADDRESS IN B.C. (NOT P.O. BOX)
123 Any Street   CITY **North Vancouver**

PROVINCE **British Columbia**   POSTAL CODE **Z1P 0G0**   DATE OF ESTABLISHING BUSINESS IN B.C.   YR **9—** MO. **01** DAY **15**

NATURE OF BUSINESS
Retail Grocers

B. GENERAL PARTNERSHIP ONLY

NAME (IN FULL)
John Dean Doe

RESIDENTIAL OR REGISTERED ADDRESS (NOT P.O. BOX)
321 Yin Street

CITY **Vancouver**   PROVINCE **B.C.**   POSTAL CODE **Z1P 0G0**

NAME (IN FULL)
Jean Jane Doe

RESIDENTIAL OR REGISTERED ADDRESS (NOT P.O. BOX)
321 Yin Street

CITY **Vancouver**   PROVINCE **B.C.**   POSTAL CODE **Z1P 0G0**

DATE OF REGISTRATION

NAME (IN FULL)

RESIDENTIAL OR REGISTERED ADDRESS (NOT P.O. BOX)

CITY   PROVINCE   POSTAL CODE

NAME (IN FULL)

RESIDENTIAL OR REGISTERED ADDRESS (NOT P.O. BOX)

CITY   PROVINCE   POSTAL CODE

IF ANY PARTNER IS A CORPORATION, STATE PRINCIPAL PLACE OF BUSINESS IN B.C. (ADDRESS)

SIGNATURE OF PARTNER

SIGNATURE OF PARTNER *John Dean Doe*

SIGNATURE OF PARTNER *Jean Jane Doe*

SIGNATURE OF PARTNER

CERTIFICATION
I HEREBY CERTIFY THAT THE PERSONS NAMED IN THIS DECLARATION ARE THE ONLY MEMBERS OF THE PARTNERSHIP.

C. PROPRIETORSHIP ONLY

NAME (IN FULL)

RESIDENTIAL OR REGISTERED ADDRESS (NOT P.O. BOX)

CITY   PROVINCE   POSTAL CODE

IF A CORPORATION, STATE PRINCIPAL PLACE OF BUSINESS IN B.C. (ADDRESS)

SIGNATURE OF PROPRIETOR

CERTIFICATION. I HEREBY CERTIFY THAT NO OTHER PERSON IS ASSOCIATED WITH ME IN THIS PROPRIETORSHIP.

D. LIMITED PARTNERSHIP ONLY

ADDRESS OF REGISTERED OFFICE IN B.C.

CITY   PROVINCE   POSTAL CODE

JURISDICTION WHERE LIMITED PARTNERSHIP FORMED

IF LIMITED PARTNERSHIP FORMED OUT OF B.C. STATE NAME AND ADDRESS OF GENERAL PARTNER(S)

SIGNATURE

RELATIONSHIP TO LIMITED PARTNERSHIP

CERTIFICATION
I HEREBY CERTIFY THAT THE PERSONS ON THE ATTACHED CERTIFICATE ARE THE ONLY MEMBERS OF THE LIMITED PARTNERSHIP.

RC 101-83

In addition, partners are fully liable, jointly and individually, for debts incurred by each other while acting in the course of business, regardless of the proportionate capital contribution of the individual parties. And be warned — you may be considered to be in partnership with someone even though you have not filed a formal Declaration of Partnership form at the office of the Registrar of Companies in Victoria. This is because, legally, a partnership is created by the relationship of the parties and not by any formal act or documents signed by the parties. There is no established test as to what constitutes a partnership, although the following questions offer some guidelines.

(a) Is there a sharing of net profits and losses?

(b) Do any of the parties act as agents for the others?

(c) Is there any property held in joint tenancy?

(d) Is there any implication of partnership on your firm's letterhead or in its correspondence?

(e) Is the nature of the work relationship that of a partnership?

b. CORPORATIONS

Many people prefer to carry on business as a corporation because of the unique characteristics of a corporate entity. A corporation is a distinct legal entity, an "artificial person" quite separate from the people who are its shareholders. When you incorporate, you actually create a new person in the eyes of the law. The assets and debts of a corporation belong to it — not to the individual shareholders.

1. Advantages to incorporating

Because of the characteristics outlined above, there are four major advantages for people who incorporate their businesses.

(a) Greater source of capital

There is potentially a greater source of capital available than in a partnership or proprietorship. Since the company is an entity separate from its shareholders, people may invest money in it without accepting any further responsibility for conducting the company business and without worrying about becoming liable for the debts of the company.

(b) Perpetual existence

Since the company is a separate entity, it does not expire when the shareholders die. Substantial estate planning benefits result from this aspect of incorporation.

(c) Limited liability

This is the main reason businesses incorporate. The most advantageous and unique characteristic of a company is its limited liability, and this is why corporations are referred to as "limited companies." The words "Limited" or "Ltd.," "Incorporated" or "Inc.," "Corporation" or "Corp." must appear in the names of all companies and must *not* appear in the name of a proprietorship or partnership. This very special concept is contained in section 55(3) of the Company Act which simply states:

> No member of a company is personally liable for the debts, obligations, or acts of the company.

This means that your liability as a shareholder is limited to the amount of money you owe the company (i.e., for shares), and does not include the amounts of money that the company itself owes to its creditors. This is obviously an important advantage.

There are, however, certain limitations, the most important being that, in many instances, creditors, particularly banks, will not extend credit to a small company without your personal guarantee as its shareholder. (A bank may also require the corporation's owners to take out life insurance as a condition to obtaining a loan. The type of insurance involved is almost always term insurance, but the important point to remember is that the premium on this type of transaction is a *company* expense. If you have paid for this personally, you are entitled to be reimbursed by the company.)

However, if you do not personally guarantee your company's loans, your liability as a shareholder is limited to what you have invested in the company and the amount you owe for unpaid shares, if any. The following examples illustrate these principles.

Example 1

John Doe and Jack Doe carry on business as a partnership known as J & J Industries.

J & J Industries incurs debts of $25 000.

The assets of J & J Industries are $10 000.

A creditor successfully petitions J & J Industries into bankruptcy or simply gets a judgment against J & J Industries.

All the assets of John Doe and Jack Doe, as individuals, including possibly their homes, cars, etc., may be executed against to repay the $15 000 debt incurred by the partnership over and above its assets.

Example 2

John Doe and Jack Doe carry on business as a corporation known as J & J Industries Limited, with John Doe and Jack Doe the only shareholders, each having purchased one share at $1 (although any number of shares can be purchased).

J & J Industries Limited incurs debts of $25 000.

The assets of J & J Industries Limited are considered to have a market value of $10 000.

A creditor successfully petitions J & J Industries Limited into bankruptcy.

The creditors can realize $10 000 on the assets of the company but they have no rights against John and Jack as individuals,* regardless of the value of personal assets that John and Jack may own outside the company.

The creditors are creditors of the company, not of John and Jack.

(d) Community recognition

An incorporated company usually has more credibility in the eyes of banks, creditors, and customers. If you have gone to the trouble and expense of incorporating, indicating that you have long-range plans for your business, you are taken seriously.

(e) Tax advantages

The potential tax advantages of incorporating are so important that a whole chapter has been devoted to the subject (see chapter 2).

2. Disadvantages to incorporating

There are, however, disadvantages to incorporating that you should consider. First, operating through a company does entail extra paperwork. You have to file incorporation documents, notices, and annual reports. You have to file two tax returns: one for your company and one for yourself. You must maintain proper accounting records. Section 195 of the Company Act, the act that regulates corporations, states:

Accounting records required.

195. (1) Every company shall keep proper accounting records in respect of all financial and other transactions of the company, and, without limiting the generality of the foregoing, shall keep records of

(a) every sum of money received and disbursed by the company and the matters in respect of which the receipt and disbursement takes place;

(b) every sale and purchase by the company;

(c) every asset and liability of the company; and

(d) every other transaction affecting the financial position of the company.

(2) The accounting records of a company shall be kept at a place determined by the directors, but the Registrar may order that they be kept within the Province.

(3) The accounting records of a company shall be open to the inspection of any director during the normal business hours of the company.

---

*The general exception to this rule is that, as directors of a company, Jack and John remain personally liable for the debts of the company in respect of wages and commissions due employees.

5

(4) Subject to the articles or an ordinary resolution, the directors may determine to what extent, at which times and places, and under what conditions the accounting records of the company shall be open to the inspection of members.

(5) Every company that contravenes any requirement of this section is guilty of an offence.

There may also be additional government paperwork to do from time to time. Also, there is the cost of setting up and maintaining a minute book and records office (see chapter 5) and your duties as a director (see chapter 12).

Second, if the company has an income of more than $200 000 per year, you actually pay significantly higher taxes than if you were not incorporated. However, I assume this situation applies to so few companies that further comment is unnecessary.

Third, there is the cost and bother of doing the incorporating. By the time you are finished, you will have spent $300 to $400 and a few hours of your time.

c. SUMMARY OF WAYS OF CARRYING ON BUSINESS

As discussed above, there are three main legal forms an organization can take. These forms and their characteristics are outlined briefly below for quick reference.

Proprietorship

(a) Unincorporated

(b) Owned by one person

(c) Creditors have a legal claim on both the investment in the business and the personal assets of the owner.

Partnership

(a) Unincorporated

(b) Each partner has unlimited liability in a general partnership arrangement.

(c) The acts of one partner in the course of the management of the business are binding upon the other partners.

(d) The partnership dissolves upon the death or withdrawal of any partner, or upon the acceptance of a new partner.

Incorporated company

(a) Incorporated in most provinces by Memorandum of Association or federally by Articles of Incorporation

(b) Exists as a separate legal entity

(c) Shareholders are liable only to the extent of their investment and callable shares they hold in the corporation (callable shares are those that are not fully paid for)

(d) Usually possesses tax advantages

d. FINANCIAL STATEMENTS AND THEIR IMPORTANCE

No matter what legal form an organization takes, the preparation of meaningful financial statements is vital because various people will have an interest in the financial affairs of the organization, namely, owners, managers, creditors, Revenue Canada, and prospective buyers.

To illustrate, let us assume that you are a bank manager and that J & J Industries Limited, a medium-sized corporation in the business of manufacturing, approaches you for a $10 000 loan. The principals explain that the funds are necessary for plant expansion. As a prospective creditor, you would be interested in two things: the ability of J & J Industries Limited to pay the regular instalments of principal and interest on the loan and the amount the bank would recover if the company could not meet its obligation.

To satisfy your curiosity, you would have to examine the financial statements of the company. The annual income would be shown on the profit and loss, or income and expense, statement. This figure, if compared with the income statement from prior periods, would indicate to you the rate of economic growth of the enterprise.

In addition you would be able to determine whether or not enough total revenue is generated to repay the proposed loan. The balance sheet of the company would indicate any other long-term debt for which the company is liable. Furthermore, you would be able to determine which assets (inventories, accounts receivable, etc.) are available as security for the proposed loan.

The company's ability to pay its current obligations is another important indicator of the economic health of the enterprise. This ability to pay present debts when due can also be determined from the balance sheet. This indicator is expressed as a ratio (called the "current ratio") and is calculated by dividing the total current assets by the total current liabilities. This is illustrated in Sample #3. Current assets exceed current liabilities in the ratio of 2:1. In other words, the working capital position of the company in this case is healthy.

In summary, you would obtain much of the information so vital to your decision regarding the loan by looking at the financial statements of J & J Industries Limited.

The preceding illustration shows how financial statements can be useful to potential creditors. Furthermore, financial statements are useful to anyone who has an interest (monetary or otherwise) in an enterprise. Just as certain medical implements are the tools by which a doctor can get some indication of physical health, so financial statements are the tools by which interested parties can measure the economic health of an organization.

Below is a breakdown, in point form, of the three major financial statements: the balance sheet, the profit and loss statement, and the earned surplus statement. They are discussed here to enable you to get some idea of the function and contents of financial statements.

1. Balance sheet

The balance sheet is a position statement, not a historical record; it shows what is owed at a given date. There are three sections to a balance sheet: assets, liabilities, and statement of retained earnings (see Sample #4).

SAMPLE #3
BALANCE SHEET (Partial)

J & J INDUSTRIES LIMITED

March 31, 199-

Current Assets

Cash	$ 20 000
Accounts receivable	290 000
Inventories	90 000
TOTAL	$400 000

Current Liabilities

Trade payables	$100 000
Wages payable	10 000
Current portion of long term debt	90 000
TOTAL	$200 000

(a) Assets

Current assets are those assets that will be used up within one year of the current balance sheet date. Normal valuation of such assets is at original cost or market value, whichever is lower.

Fixed assets are those assets that provide benefits to the organization over a longer period than one year from the current balance sheet date. Valuation is generally at original cost less accumulated depreciation. The amount of depreciation is based on the length of the useful life of the asset and the original cost of the asset.

To illustrate:

Building: original cost $40 000

Useful life: 20 years

Portion of asset cost which expires in each period:

$$\frac{\$40\ 000}{20} = \$2\ 000$$

This type of depreciation is normally calculated on a reducing balance basis but for this illustration I have used the straight-line method. The sum of $2 000 is charged to the profit and loss statement in each period and is accumulated on the balance sheet as a reduction of the original cost of the asset. Thus, five years after the building was purchased, the balance sheet would show:

Building, at cost	$40 000
Less accumulated depreciation	
(5 x 2000)	10 000
Book value of building	$30 000

Because the asset may be sold for more than the original cost, the book value does not necessarily indicate the amount the equity-holders should receive for their ownership of the building. (**Note:** the "equity-holders" in a company are the shareholders.)

(b) Liabilities and owners' equity

Liabilities are those things that are owed by the company to others, on both a short-term and a long-term basis, and include such things as accounts payable, bank loans, and unpaid taxes.

Owners' equity is determined by subtracting liabilities from total assets and represents the value of the owners' shareholding for accounting purposes. This value may very well be different from the fair market value of the owners' shareholdings because fair market value can only be determined from what an arm's length purchaser would be prepared to pay for the shareholdings, and not necessarily what the shareholdings are valued at for accounting purposes.

2. Profit and loss statement

This statement indicates the profit or loss by subtracting the total expenses for that period from the total revenue for that period. There are two ways of determining when revenue is earned and when expenses are incurred, the cash basis method and the accrual basis method. In the cash basis method no revenue is recognized until cash is received. No expenses are recognized until cash is disbursed. If, on the other hand, accounting is done on the accrual basis, revenue is recognized as soon as it is earned. Expenses are recognized as soon as they are incurred. The actual receipt or disbursement of cash is irrelevant.

3. Statement of retained earnings

The statement of retained earnings is a statement showing accumulated retained earnings from year to year. Added to the opening balance of retained earnings for the year is the current year's net profit (after income taxes are paid). From that sum, dividends declared and paid are subtracted to arrive at a closing balance for the current year.

The closing balance is summarized on the balance sheet in Sample #4 as the entry Retained Earnings and Partners' Equity. The closing balance for the current year becomes the opening balance for the following year.

SAMPLE #4
BALANCE SHEET FOR UNINCORPORATED BUSINESS

ASSETS

Current Assets

Cash on hand and in bank		720.12	
Accounts receivable less allowance for doubtful accounts		657.72	
Merchandise inventory valued at the lower of original cost or market		3 212.63	
Prepaid expenses		157.55	
Total current assets			$ 4 748.02

Fixed Assets — At Cost

Land		2 320.00	
Building	$5 767.16		
Less: accumulated depreciation	1 727.92	4 039.24	
Store fixtures	3 726.12		
Less: accumulated depreciation	982.36	2 743.76	
Delivery truck	2 760.20		
Less: accumulated depreciation	513.60	2 246.60	11 349.60
			16 097.62

LIABILITIES & PARTNERS' EQUITY

Current Liabilities

Trade Accounts payable	$2 772.58	
Accrued wage	75.20	
Employees' income tax payable	60.16	
Accrued real estate taxes	220.00	
Total current liabilities		3 127.54

Retained Earnings and Partners' Equity*

Jones's share	$6 484.84	
Smith's share	6 484.84	
		12 969.68
		$16 097.62

*If the company was incorporated, this would read as follows:

Issued and fully paid for:
Jones — 50 shares at $1.00 = $50.00
Smith — 50 shares at $1.00 = $50.00

CAPITAL STOCK
Common stock, no par value — 100 shares.
Retained earnings $12 969.68

2

LIMIT YOURSELF TO LIMIT TAXES

There can be substantial tax advantages to incorporating your business. This section outlines the major ones.

a. BASIC CORPORATE RATE*

The basic combined federal and provincial corporate income tax rate before the small business deduction and manufacturing and processing credit is approximately 44%. The rate on income from manufacturing operations is about 36%.

b. QUALIFYING FOR THE SMALL BUSINESS TAX RATE*

Provided your business can qualify for the small business rate, you can receive a substantial reduction in taxes payable on business earnings. The rate for the first $200 000 of all net income from active business is about 22%.

To qualify for the small business rate on the first $200 000 of net income from an active business, there are certain tests to meet:

(a) Your corporation must be a Canadian-controlled private corporation; that is, a private Canadian corporation other than a corporation controlled directly or indirectly by one or more non-residents or by one or more public corporations or by any such combination.

(b) Your company must generate income from an active business in Canada.

(c) Corporations that are "associated" with the corporation in question have not claimed the small business tax rate.

If the corporation fails these tests, then the tax rate will be between approximately 31% and 46% depending on whether the income is from manufacturing and processing or not.

Any business carried on by your corporation will be considered active with two exceptions: personal services businesses (which refers to personal services that would ordinarily be provided by an individual employee rather than by a company) and investment businesses. Personal service corporations are held ineligible in order to prevent an individual who incorporates to obtain the benefit of lower taxes when, in fact, he or she could be considered an "employee" of the company paying remuneration. This type of corporation usually has income from one main source and has less than five employees. If you are contemplating forming a personal service corporation, you should obtain professional advice.

Personal services businesses and investment businesses will be taxed at the higher rate unless the company has six or more full-time employees throughout the year or if, in the case of a management services company, it receives its income from a corporation associated with it. In such cases, investment companies and "incorporated employees" will both be eligible for the low tax rate.

Assuming you qualify for the small business rate, the tax advantages to incorporating are outlined below.

---

*All rates depend on the province in which you reside and whether the provincial corporate rates remain as they are.

c. MINIMIZE NON-DEDUCTIBLE OR DEPRECIABLE EXPENSES

By doing your own incorporation, you will realize an immediate tax saving in addition to saving on actual costs. As lawyers' fees are not wholly tax deductible as an expense, by doing it yourself you not only save the lawyer's fees, you avoid paying taxes on a non-deductible expense.

d. SPLIT YOUR INCOME

With a company, you can effectively "split" your income. For example, say your business made $75 000 last year as a proprietorship. This entire amount would be considered your personal income and be taxed at the top rate of up to about 51%.*

On the other hand, if you have incorporated, $25 000 could be paid to you personally as salary or bonus and $50 000 could be left in the company. This $50 000 would be taxed at the rate of 22% if your company qualifies for the small business tax rate.

On the $25 000 paid out to you personally, you would pay tax in the 8% to 32% range, depending on the number of personal deductions, etc., you have. The top personal marginal rate will be between 47% and 51% depending on the province you live in.

This is just one example. In fact, you are allowed to work out any combination that keeps your total tax bill to a minimum, including employing members of your family, provided they are employed in a bona fide capacity and the payment is reasonable.

At present, a qualifying company's tax rate is only 22% on all earnings below $200 000 per year. Therefore, if your company's earnings are $50 000 a year, you will pay only 22% in taxes each year.

A further split is also possible. After paying this initial corporate tax, you can then choose to either leave the funds in the company or pay out dividends to the shareholders (which might be, for example, you, your spouse, and children).

Depending upon other sources of income and your personal income tax bracket, it may be more advantageous for one or more of your family members to take payments from the company in the form of dividends alone or in a mixture of dividends and salary. An individual (other than a resident of Quebec) with no other sources of income will be able to receive approximately $22 000 of Canadian dividends without being subject to tax. This is because of the dividend tax credit. The company must be carefully structured for this technique to work properly.

However, since dividends are not deductible and it is important to limit, if at all possible, net corporate business income to $200 000 in order to pay the lowest corporate income tax rate, payments of bonuses and salary may be preferable to dividends.

One critical point to keep in mind is that dividend income does not qualify as "earned income" for purposes of making a deductible contribution to an RRSP. Thus, if your entire income consisted of dividends, you could not get a deduction for any contribution to your RRSP. Furthermore, your income might also be subject to the new minimum tax.

e. ESTATE PLANNING BENEFITS

With a company, you can effect substantial estate planning advantages. As this is a technical area and beyond the scope of this book, it will not be discussed at any length. Suffice it to say that the existence of a company enables you to own a widely diversified portfolio of assets (including all kinds of property) under the ownership of a single entity.

This can be a great advantage from both a tax and an administrative point of view, especially if the company is located in a non-inheritance tax jurisdiction (e.g.,

---

*This rate may be greater or less depending on the province in which you reside.

Alberta or British Columbia) and the assets are located in an inheritance tax jurisdiction (e.g., Washington state).

f. SALARY AND BONUS ACCRUALS

Through a company, you can declare yourself a bonus that is deductible from the company's income but need not be declared by you as income until it is actually paid. However, the Income Tax Act has rules about how long you can delay declaring the payment as income to you. The rules say that the bonus has to be taken within 180 days from the end of your corporation's tax year in which the bonus was declared. For example, if your company's year end was January 31 and you declared yourself a bonus of $10 000 on January 30, 1996, the company would deduct it as a salary expense for the 1995-96 year only if the bonus was actually paid by July 31, 1996.

The result is that you would pay personal tax on the bonus in April 1995 (less, of course, the tax the company would have to withhold when it paid you the bonus).

You can see that this gives you some flexibility. To be deductible, these bonuses must be reasonable (in relation to services rendered to the company) and represent a legal liability of the company. (Passing a directors' resolution is adequate.) In addition, there are a number of other tax wrinkles and elections relating to the salary/dividend/bonus route that any competent tax adviser can tell you about.

The important thing to remember is that you must be careful in planning bonuses to look at the overall tax liability of you and your company. If your company is already able to take advantage of the low small business tax rate, there is little sense in declaring a bonus that will be taxed in your hands as personal income at a slightly higher rate.

If you want to reduce your company's earnings so that it can take advantage of the small business rate, you might want to declare a bonus payable to yourself and wait before paying it to yourself. In this way you can "even out" the earnings and so pay less total tax.

For example, if you can foresee that your company's earnings for the fiscal year will exceed the amount eligible for the small business tax rate, declare a bonus for yourself, as it may reduce the earnings sufficiently to enable the company to be taxed at the lower small business rate, or mean less money is taxable at a higher rate. Note that if you do decide to declare yourself a bonus, it must be paid to you no longer than six months after year end.

Furthermore, by reducing your corporate profits, you reduce the size of the tax instalment payments payable by the corporation and, therefore, improve your cashflow position.

If you declare dividends payable to yourself, there is no time limit on when they can be paid to you. Once the corporation has paid tax on its profits, dividends can be distributed at any time. This might be beneficial from the point of view of liability for personal income tax.

Remember, whichever method you choose to distribute your corporate earnings, it must be designed to meet the monetary needs and tax liability of both you and the company.

g. EXPENSE DEDUCTIONS

Aside from the fact that operating your business through a limited company may allow you to claim more liberal travel and entertainment expenses, there are perfectly legal and sanctioned ways of using a company to increase expense allowances. For example, country club and similar dues paid by your company on your behalf, while not tax deductible by the company, do not have to be included in your personal income, provided you use the clubs for business entertainment. Therefore, because the company is taxed at a lower rate than you personally, it can earn less than you to net the same amount.

However, business meals and entertainment are only deductible to 80% of their cost. The cost of business meals and entertainment subject to the 80% limitation includes gratuities, overcharges, room rentals at a hotel to provide entertainment, and tickets for entertainment events.

Similarly, if you are arranging life insurance policies, the company can pay the premiums (non-deductible — but the money earned to pay the premium is taxed at a lower rate) and any proceeds collected by the company are non-taxable.

h. PLANNING FOR RETIREMENT

In the past, the opportunity for small business owners to provide for their own retirement was exceptional. Unfortunately, that is no longer the case.

If you are an owner/employee of a corporation, you may not be a beneficiary of your corporation's DPSP. If the company does not have a deferred profit-sharing plan (DPSP) or a registered pension plan (RPP), or you are not a beneficiary, your maximum contribution to a registered retirement savings plan can be 18% of your earned income, up to specified limits.

Under pension reform, your RRSP dollar limits will increase over time for an individual who is not a member of a DPSP or an RPP and are as follows:

1995 — $15 500

1996 — $13 500

1997 — $13 500

1998 — $14 500

1999 — $15 500

Retiring allowances given to employees or employee/shareholders can be transferred to an RRSP, but are limited to $3 500 for each year the employee did not have vested rights under an RPP or DPSP and $2 000 for each year the employee did have such vested benefits. For years of service commencing in 1989, the transfer is limited to $2 000 per year of service.

i. LOANS TO EMPLOYEES AND SHAREHOLDERS

Loans made by a corporation to employees that have a below market rate of interest or are non-interest bearing will create a taxable benefit to the employee. The taxable benefit will be equal to the difference between the interest rate charged to the employee and the "prescribed" loan rate set by the government.

This rate is adjusted quarterly based on the interest rate paid on 91-day treasury bills for the previous quarter. In other words, on a no-interest loan of $10 000, $1 400 is added to the employee's income.

However, on loans to purchase shares in their employer company, employees will be able to deduct the interest expense against all other employment income or income from property and dividends, provided the shares bought are either preferred shares that yield taxable dividends higher than the prescribed interest rate or common shares. Thus, no net benefit will be included in the employee's income. It should be noted, however, that to the extent that an employee's interest expense exceeds income from property (e.g., interest and dividends, etc.) it will effectively reduce any immediate access to the capital gains exemption by the amount of such excess until such excess is ultimately absorbed by income from property.

Where the loan is made to allow the employee to buy a car to be used on the job, the maximum deduction for interest costs is $250 per month. However, in order to deduct this maximum interest amount, you must drive your car no less than 24 000 kilometres per year. There are very complex rules pertaining to the deduction of automobile expenses and your professional advisers should be consulted.

To summarize, low-interest or no-interest loans to employees are no longer as beneficial as they once were unless they are made to allow the employee to buy shares of the employer company. Loans to allow an employee to buy a car can also be beneficial, but not to the same extent.

j. MANUFACTURING AND PROCESSING CREDIT (M & P)

All active small business income will be taxed at the same rate and the rates on such income will range from about 16% to 22%, depending on the province in which your company resides. For income not eligible for the small business rate, the M & P credit will reduce the rate of tax on manufacturing income not eligible for the small business rate from about 31% to 42%, depending on the province in which your company resides.

The M & P credit was introduced to reward labor-intensive businesses, supposedly as a stimulus to employment. The Income Tax Act specifically disqualifies certain activities. They are farming, fishing, logging, on-site job construction, most natural resource activities, and any manufacturing endeavor where manufacturing revenues are less than 10% of the gross sales. Businesses that convert, change, add to, or re-assemble the raw material may qualify. For example, newspapers or printing businesses qualify. Restaurants qualify because they process food.

If your business is primarily manufacturing and processing in Canada, did not carry on active business outside the country in the year, and did not carry on activities specifically excluded from the definition of manufacturing and processing, all of your company's income qualifies for this credit so long as its income does not exceed $22 000.

k. ANTI-AVOIDANCE

The general anti-avoidance rule (GAAR) states that any transaction that results in a significant reduction or even deferral of the tax that might have been payable had the transaction not occurred can be completely ignored unless it can be shown to have had a bona fide non-tax purpose. This rule will not be applied to prohibit access to certain specified tax incentives, including the small business deduction and the manufacturing and processing tax credit. Therefore, a business person is free to use a corporate vehicle to access these special tax incentives.

l. CONCLUSION

The realization that profits mean taxes tends to cause business people to overreact and become more and more committed to minimizing their tax load. This is totally understandable and perfectly acceptable, as long as the methods used do not cause the tax tail to wag the dog and are legal.

The best way to achieve the lowest taxes is to maintain proper and accurate records and ensure that you have at your disposal the legal and accounting expertise you require to assist you in taking advantage of all of the opportunities available under the current tax laws.

3
PRELIMINARY MATTERS

a. WHERE TO INCORPORATE

Since a company is an artificial person, it must be created by someone. A company may be incorporated or "born" because of a federal charter, Articles of Incorporation, or by a provincial certificate.

The main advantages of incorporating federally are that the corporation is empowered to carry on business in all provinces, provided it becomes registered in each province in which it carries on business, and it can use the same name in each province even if there is already a company using a similar name.

The disadvantages are the higher initial cost and the amount of yearly paper work that must be done to keep up to date on all filings required by the provinces and the federal Director of the Corporations Branch. It will cost you over $500 to incorporate federally and, if you hire a lawyer, it will cost more.

For these reasons it is easier for most private companies that are owned and operated by a small family group or group of business associates to incorporate in one province and then register in successive provinces as they wish to expand. Usually there is no problem in becoming registered in a new province.

This book deals with incorporating a private, non-reporting corporation in the province of British Columbia only. If you are interested in incorporating federally or in another province, please refer to the appropriate incorporation guide in the Self-Counsel Series. Self-Counsel also publishes incorporation guides for Washington and Oregon for those interested in doing business in the United States.

b. NON-REPORTING vs. REPORTING COMPANIES

Until recently, all companies could be classified as "private" or "public." Public companies were commonly the larger companies whose shares were traded on stock exchanges. Private companies were the average, small, family-owned companies, probably more accurately referred to as "incorporated partnerships."

This terminology has been abolished and the distinction is now made between "reporting" and "non-reporting" companies. Generally, these terms mean the same as the old definitions of public and private companies.

1. Reporting companies

Section 1(1) of the Company Act states:

"reporting company" means a corporation incorporated by or under an Act of the Legislature other than a corporation continued under section 37

(a) that has any of its securities listed for trading on any stock exchange wheresoever situate;

(b) that is ordered by the registrar to be a reporting company; or

(c) that

(i) was or was deemed to be a public company immediately before October 1, 1973;

(ii) had obtained an exemption order, under section 38A of the Act repealed by this Act, where the exemption order was in effect immediately before October 1, 1973;

(iii) with respect to any of its securities, files a prospectus with the Superintendent of Brokers and obtains a receipt for it; or

(iv) became an amalgamated company after October 1, 1973 if one of the amalgamating companies was, at the time of the amalgamation, a reporting company,

unless the registrar orders that it is not a reporting company;

The significance of this section is that there are no longer any hard and fast rules defining what a "public" company is and what it is not. The Superintendent of Brokers now has the freedom to consider you a reporting (public) company no matter how many shareholders you have. It all depends on the conduct of the company.

The directors on the board of a reporting company usually consist of a group of respected business people who bring to the board a wide variety of business experience. Their function is to act as "watchdogs" over the officers and to protect the interests of the shareholders who elect them on an annual basis. Unfortunately, for a variety of reasons, this objective is not always attained.

Most officers of large reporting companies are "hired professionals" who are in charge of the day-to-day activities. In many companies they also wield the greatest influence on the overall operations of the company. Usually the two or three top officers of the company are also members of the board of directors.

The last group in a reporting company, but certainly the largest in terms of numbers, consists of shareholders. In reporting companies, shareholders are the theoretical "owners" of the company which, in turn, owns the assets. Shares represent ownership. However, ownership of shares does not usually vest in the shareholder the right or power to run the company. (**Note:** The term "shareholder" is interchangeable with the term "member;" both mean the same thing. Shareholders are always referred to as members in the Company Act of British Columbia.)

In theory, the final authority for a company's operations rests with the shareholders. In reality, this is often untrue. Shareholders of a reporting company are often spread all over the country, so very few attend the annual meeting. Most shareholders want only a return on their investment (dividends) and an increase in value of their shares; they do not want to run a company. If the company does not perform satisfactorily, the shareholders rarely call the management or directors to task or replace them. The shares may simply be sold.

Furthermore, many shareholders lack the competence and experience to run the business properly so they hesitate to question the activities of managing officers or directors. Also, the usual wide dispersal of shareholders means that it would take a great deal of time, money, and effort for a group of reform-minded individuals to obtain enough support to seriously challenge the management or directors of the company.

The structure of a reporting company can be represented by this diagram:

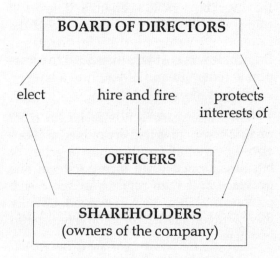

XYZ LTD.

All companies must have directors, officers, and shareholders. One distinction between reporting and non-reporting companies is that in reporting companies these positions are occupied by different persons.

A vice-president in a reporting company will not necessarily be on the board of directors, and will almost certainly not own enough shares of the company to affect corporate policy from a shareholder's position.

The vice-president's effect on the operations of the company depends solely on his or her position as an officer of the company.

2. Non-reporting companies

Obviously, not all businesses incorporate with the intention of selling shares to the public to raise large amounts of capital. To give small businesses the advantages of incorporation, a different type of company, the non-reporting company, was created by both provincial and federal legislation.

The essential characteristics of a non-reporting company in British Columbia are as follows:

(a) There is some restriction on the transfer of shares.

(b) You cannot offer for sale to the public shares or debentures of the company.

(c) The directors, officers, and shareholders are often the same people.

(d) Only one director is required, whereas a reporting company must have three.

A circular issued by the Superintendent of Brokers states the position of the Securities Commission about non-reporting companies.

It is our opinion those concepts (of a non-reporting company) must incorporate at least the following principles:

(a) The stock of the company is held in relatively few hands.

(b) The stock is not traded in securities markets.

(c) The stock is subject to restrictions on transfer.

(d) The Company has never made an offering of its securities to the public.

(e) Management and ownership are substantially identical, i.e., a community of relationship exists based upon a family, business, social, or other relationship.

We wish to point out, however, that the overriding factor the Commission must weigh when considering applications for non-reporting status, even though all of the ingredients of a "close corporation" exist in the applicant company, is the shareholders' and public's need and right to know what is transpiring in the company.

Clauses (a), (b), and (d) are self-explanatory. Clause (c) is recognition of the fact that small companies operate like partnerships and, as such, need control over who becomes a "partner" — that is, a shareholder. Therefore, some sort of restriction on the transfer of shares is needed in the case of a small company.

If you look in the model set of articles in Sample #7, you will see that the share transfer restriction is contained in part 24. This clause combines the need for control over transferability with the protection needed by a "partner" (shareholder) who wishes to sell out and receive a fair market price for his or her shares.

As you can see, a share transfer restriction is really a double-edged sword. If some other shareholder were attempting to sell his or her shares, you would like to see severe restriction on transferability to avoid the intrusion of an unwanted "partner." However, if it were *you* who wanted to sell, the fewer restrictions on transferability the better, because you could approach many more buyers.

The structure of a non-reporting corporation can be accurately described as an "incorporated partnership" because it usually consists of one, two, or three people who are close friends, business associates, or family members.

Each individual may hold two or three positions in the company. It is not unusual for one person to be, at the same time, a shareholder, officer, and director. For example, if you have a "family" company in which the husband has 50% of the shares, the wife 25%, and a son the other 25%, it is likely that these persons will be the only directors. They will then also act as the officers. Quite often both the husband and wife will be the sole directors as well as shareholders. In this case, usually both are directors, officers, and shareholders. Be careful not to confuse the duties and responsibilities of shareholder, officer, and director, even when the persons occupying these positions are the same.

The annual general meeting of a non-reporting company is one of many instances when you will wear more than one hat at the same time. For example, in the daily activities of your business, you function as an officer. If you decide, however, to branch out into a new area, or to purchase or sell company assets, you are wearing the hat of a director, as all officers must refer important matters to the board of directors. When you attend the annual meeting and vote on the issue, purchase, or sale of shares or of substantially all of the assets of the company, you function as a shareholder. Shareholders always have the last say on any issue seriously affecting the nature of the company because the shareholders are the owners of the company.

In many companies, the partners in business are not 50-50 owners when it comes to ownership of shares. This puts the minority shareholder (who holds less than 50% of the shares) in a precarious position with regard to the majority shareholder (who holds more than 50% of the shares). Ideally, if you are involved in a "two-person" corporation where the parties are not family relations, the shareholdings should be equal. If this cannot be done, the minority shareholder should obtain competent legal advice to protect his or her interest. Furthermore, if one partner is transferring substantial assets to the company, professional advice should be obtained.

You might ask what will happen if the shares are divided equally and the "partners" disagree over a basic issue and a deadlock results. The answer is that either the assets are sold and the business is wound up or one party buys out the other.

(See chapter 9 for more information.) This reflects the basic nature of a non-reporting company as an "incorporated partnership." When partners in a business have irreconcilable differences, the partnership must be dissolved. The same is true in a small company. But an equal split of the shares encourages co-operation. When this balance is altered it will, of necessity, affect the relationship of the "partners."

To avoid this problem, some companies provide for what is called a "casting vote" provision in their articles, which gives the chairperson of the meeting or the president a second casting vote in a deadlock. Frequently, however, a casting vote provision merely aggravates the dispute rather than resolves it.

c. ONE-PERSON COMPANIES

In British Columbia, the Company Act allows the formation of one-person companies. This means that the same person may be all of the following: the president, secretary, sole director, and sole shareholder, as long as that person resides in British Columbia.

The evolution of one-person companies recognizes that many people are in business solely with and for themselves (the so-called incorporated proprietorship). Rather than have a "nominal" second shareholder who performs no real function and serves no purpose, it was considered desirable to allow a single person to gain the advantages of incorporation.

The procedures for incorporation are the same for the one-person company as for any other company.

d. N.P.L. (SPECIALLY LIMITED) COMPANIES

The British Columbia Company Act also provides for a special category of companies called the Specially Limited Company or Non-Personal Liability (N.P.L.) Company.

The term "non-personal liability" is misleading in the sense that all companies, not just N.P.L. companies, provide limited liability for their shareholders, but N.P.L. companies are different from other companies in the following ways:

(a) N.P.L. companies are restricted to high-risk ventures such as exploring for, developing and mining, or producing minerals, coal, petroleum, and natural gas.

(b) Shares of N.P.L. companies can be sold at a greater discount from their par value shares at a discount. In the case of the regular company, this discount is limited to 25%, but there is no limit on the size of the discount on the price of shares in an N.P.L. company.

The N.P.L. companies can sell shares at any discount because the mining, oil, and gas industries are very risky and require a great deal of capital in order to produce any return at all. Consequently, the promoters are allowed to raise capital by selling the shares at greatly varying prices.

Unfortunately, promoters can and do abuse this privilege. One of the more common gimmicks they use is to offer shares at so-called discounts from par value, representing these shares as being offered at special discount prices. This is misleading, as the term "par value" is even more meaningless in an N.P.L. company than in an ordinary limited company. You should be wary of "friends" who offer you shares in an N.P.L. company at a special discount. Chances are nil that you would actually be getting a "deal." A company is not allowed to pay to any person a discount, commission, or allowance in exchange for his or her subscribing or agreeing to subscribe to shares.

Under the Company Act, shares without par value cannot be represented as selling at a discount because the maximum price per share concept has been eliminated as a means of determining Registrar's fees. As the Registrar now charges the same basic incorporation fee regardless of the number of without par value shares or their aggregate value, there is not even a fictional basis on which to claim that a without par value share is being sold at a discount from its "maximum selling price."

In any event, you should understand that without par value shares cannot be sold at what most consumers would call a genuine discount because the very term "without par value" means that the shares have no stated value and they are worth only whatever people will pay for them in the marketplace. Because apparent discounts are no longer allowed on without par value shares, most mining and oil companies simply use par value shares and discount them as much as they wish.

As mentioned earlier, the prime objective of most new N.P.L. mining companies is to raise enough capital to carry on some type of exploration program. This is done by floating (issuing) stock. A popular method of raising capital is to sell "cheap" stock (i.e., heavily discounted) in large blocks to investors who will, in turn, resell at higher prices. This produces a "pyramid" effect in the distribution chain. Directors often provide liberal payment terms to induce investors to buy and sell stock.

For example, there is normally a 14-day grace period between the ordering of the stock and payment for it and the directors often extend this to 60 days so the investors can resell the stock and, in effect, avoid having to pay for it themselves.

The regulations governing incorporation of an N.P.L. company are virtually the same as for a regular company with the following exceptions:

(a) The objects of such a company must be restricted to those provided in clause 2 of form 2 in the second schedule of the act. This clause states essentially that the company is restricted to doing business as described in (a) above.

(b) The name must include the words "non-personal liability" or the abbreviation "N.P.L."

(c) An N.P.L. company is restricted in its financial dealings. It cannot lend money and cannot guarantee the debts of any person or corporation. It cannot finance or help finance any other business ventures or person.

(d) The letters N.P.L. must be displayed whenever the company name is used or displayed, i.e., in all advertisements, name plates, correspondence, etc.

Because of these restrictions, most corporate lawyers today do not recommend this type of company be used at all, even for mining or oil and gas companies. In most cases, you would be just as well off with the regular corporate structure because it

(a) avoids restrictions on financial dealings,

(b) can issue par value shares at a maximum 25% discount, and

(c) can issue without par value shares at whatever price it chooses.

4
INCORPORATION PROCEDURE FOR A NON-REPORTING COMPANY IN BRITISH COLUMBIA

The following is a general, abbreviated, step-by-step list of the procedures necessary to incorporate a non-reporting company in British Columbia, with an explanation of each step. (For a checklist of these procedures, see the Appendix.)

During and after your incorporation, you will be dealing with the Registrar of Companies. The address is:

Ministry of Finance and
Corporate Relations
Corporate, Central and Mobile
Home Registry
940 Blanshard Street
Victoria, B.C. V8W 3E6
Telephone: 387-7848

The Registrar's office is open 8:30 a.m. to 4:30 p.m., Monday through Friday.

Registrar's fees are found in the Third Schedule of the Company Act, and are reprinted in Table #1 for your convenience.

Note: All documents submitted to the companies office *must* have the postal codes on all addresses.

a. GET A COPY OF THE ACT

Anyone proposing to incorporate a company should purchase a copy of the British Columbia Company Act. While many acts are difficult to understand, the Company Act is quite clearly written and is very well indexed and organized. It may be purchased

TABLE #1
INCORPORATION FEES*

Effective September 1, 1993:

For incorporation	$275
Certification of Memorandum and Articles	25
Name approval	30
For registration of an extra-provincial company	275
For filing an annual report	35
For changing the name of a British Columbia company	155
For registering a change of name of an extra-provincial company	130
For restoration of a company or an extra-provincial company to the register	305
For a certified copy of any document	25
To approve or reserve a name	30
Priority service	100

*Note that while these fees are current at the time of publication, all fees are subject to change without notice. For current fees, telephone the Registrar of Companies before submitting your documents.

from the Queen's Printer in Victoria or from the publisher. (See order form at front of book.)

b. CHOOSE A NAME

A company, like a person, must have a name, but unfortunately it is not as easy to pick a name for a company as for a baby. When you select a name for your company, you must choose a name that is acceptable not only to you but to the Registrar. In broad terms, the Registrar will usually approve a name that is not identical to and does not closely resemble any existing company names. Names that are similar to existing company names will be rejected because they may cause confusion.

With this in mind, you should try to choose a name that is both distinctive and that accurately describes the type of business you intend to carry on. For example, a name like "Quiggly Cleaners Ltd." would be a better name for a drycleaning company than "Western Enterprises Ltd." The word "Western" is one of those words that has been used in names so frequently that it is no longer distinctive. Other words with the same fate are "Northern," "Pacific," "Universal," "Maple Leaf," and many others. "Quiggly" is more distinctive.

The second element of the name, "Enterprises," does not accurately describe the business of this particular company, although it might be used more accurately in naming an investment company of some sort. "Cleaners" in the name at least gives potential customers a good idea what the company's business is.

When selecting your name, you should not use the words "Institute," "Condominium," or "Co-operative," which are restricted to specific organizations in many provinces.

Many Registrars routinely refuse to accept any names that imply a connection with or approval of the Royal Family. For this reason, names using words such as "Imperial" or "Royal" will be rejected. Furthermore, names that imply government approval or the sponsorship of a branch, service, or department are frequently not acceptable. That eliminates words such as "Parliament Hill," "R.C.M.P.," "Legislative," or "British Columbia" from the list of choices.

The Registrar will probably not approve a name that could be construed as obscene or that is too general in that it only describes the quality, goods, or function of the services. Companies with names like "General Motors" and "Best Foods" have more or less taken up these choices.

Last, but not least, stay well away from the names of companies already in existence (or the common contractions of their names). For example, a name like Xerox Construction Ltd. implies that your resources are connected with those of Xerox. This is only acceptable if true. If it is not true, Xerox may accuse you of trying to "steal" the name and bring a "passing off" suit against you.

You may also get into trouble, or at the very least have your choice rejected, if it is a name like Inco Investments Ltd. The word "Inco" is a commonly used abbreviation for the International Nickel Company and thus unacceptable.

Of course, in the case of an N.P.L. company you will also have to include the words "non-personal liability" or the abbreviation "N.P.L." This is usually in brackets at the end of the name (e.g., Drydock Mines Ltd. (N.P.L.)).

One of the easiest ways to check out existing names is to look in the telephone directory for the names of companies already doing business in your area. Trade and corporation directories, which are available in any large library, will help you find other protected names of Canadian organizations.

Generally, you should remember that the most successful proposals are likely to be —

(a) A coined word (perhaps a combination of incorporators' names) plus a descriptive word (e.g., Kenbar Dolls Ltd.).

(b) The full name of an individual (e.g., John Albert Doe Ltd.). However, be careful about using your name as the company name. First, depending on the business you are in, you may get people phoning you at home at all hours. Second, if your company goes bankrupt, you will be tarred with the same brush for many years simply because of the name. And third, if you ever sell out, your name will go with the business and somebody else might run it into the ground, with the same result as if you had gone bankrupt.

(c) The name of an individual combined with a descriptive word (e.g., Doe Explorations Ltd.).

(d) The combination of a distinctive geographic name plus a descriptive word (e.g., Fraser Valley Machinery Inc.), provided the company is connected with or operating in that area.

Of course, all names must end with "Limited," "Incorporated," or "Corporation" or the abbreviation of one of these words.

You can also use numerals as the distinctive element in your company name. A year can be part of your company name, as long as it is the year of incorporation, amalgamation, or registration, e.g., Fraser Valley Machinery (1994) Ltd.

If you want to use a number for your company name, e.g., 1234567 Enterprises Ltd., the Registrar of Companies will select one for you. You can indicate this by leaving a seven-letter space (about 1½") in front of the words "B.C. Ltd." or "British Columbia Ltd." on your memorandum and other documents wherever you need to give the name of your company (e.g., _____ B.C. Ltd.). The name given will depend on the next available number at the time of incorporation. **You do not need to reserve your name if you use this procedure.** All number names must end with "Limited," "Incorporated," or "Corporation" or the abbreviation of one of these words.

c. HAVE THE NAME RESERVED

To have your chosen name searched and reserved, submit a list of no more than three names, in order of preference, to the Registrar of Companies for approval, along with the $30 fee. You must do this by letter or by filling out the Name Approval Request form, available from the Registrar of Companies. For a copy of the form, call 356-2893 in Victoria, or 775-1044 in Greater Vancouver. Copies of the form are also available at the B.C. Access Centre or government agent nearest you.

(You cannot reserve by telephone or fax unless you have a search fee account at the Registrar of Companies, and there is no reason to open an account unless you plan to do a number of separate name reservations. If you do wish to open an account, write to the Registrar for information and an application form.)

The Registrar will reserve the approved name for 56 days and will give you a reservation number which should be quoted in your filing letter when you send in your incorporation documents. Thus, you have 56 days from the date of approval of the name to complete your incorporation. If it is not completed within that time, someone else may claim the name and you would then have to start all over again. In the event of an unforeseen delay in proceeding with incorporation, the Registrar will, for an additional fee, reserve the approved name for a further 56 days upon receipt of a request in writing.

A number company name is assigned by the Registrar at the time of incorporation. You do not need to reserve your name or pay the name reservation fee (see section **b. 1.** above).

d. PREPARE THE MEMORANDUM

The memorandum is your company's "constitution." The form of the memorandum is quite simple and is, in most cases, a one-page document. A British Columbia company does not need objectives defining the areas of business available to the company; the company has all the powers and capacities of a natural person. This means your company may engage in any sort of business that it chooses (restrictions do exist for those who wish to form trust companies, insurance companies, railway lines, and clubs).

If you wish, you may impose restrictions on your company if, for example, you wish to protect your investment funds by insisting that the company invest in mortgages only. These cases are rare, however.

You can see a completed memorandum in Sample #5. A memorandum for a non-personal liability company follows in Sample #6. You may use par value shares, or shares without par value, or both. These examples use shares without par value because they more accurately reflect the true share value than par value shares. (For more information on shares, see chapter 7.)

If you want a more complicated share structure, the rights and restrictions have to be detailed in the memorandum or articles. If they are detailed in the memorandum, the articles must explain this (see paragraph 2.1 in Sample #7). If they are contained in the articles, the description of the classes of shares in the capital clause of the memorandum should state, for example, "The class B shares and the preference shares shall have special rights and restrictions set forth in the articles of the company."

Where there are classes of common shares and the only difference between them is the right to vote, then this difference should be part of the designation of the classes in the capital clause.

The sample memorandum for the N.P.L. company reflects the fact that most companies of this sort would issue three to five million shares, while ten thousand shares would be adequate for most normal companies. Both types of companies may increase the number of shares at a later date at no extra cost if they wish to.

The two subscribers in Samples #5 and #6 have signed the memorandum and have written the number of shares each is subscribing for next to their names. If possible, you should do the same, although someone like a lawyer can incorporate the company by taking only one or two shares and then transferring them to the intended shareholders at the first meeting of directors.

If you sign the memorandum as a subscriber, you are assuming the duties and responsibilities of a director until the first meeting of the shareholders, when new directors are elected and a notice of change of directors is filed. (See chapter 12 for a discussion on directors' duties.)

Remember, the minimum number of shares you can subscribe for is one, and it is recommended, but not necessary, that the subscribers be the intended shareholders.

e. PREPARE THE ARTICLES

Your articles are the rules and regulations that govern the conduct of the company members and directors. The articles in Sample #7 are adapted for a simple non-reporting company and are available in the *Incorporation Forms for B.C.* or the software package, *Incorporation Self-Ware.* (See order form at front of book.) If you wish to adopt a set of articles *other* than that in Table A of

Form 1
(Section 5)
COMPANY ACT
MEMORANDUM

_____We_____ wish to be formed into a company with limited liablilty under the Company Act in pursuance of this Memorandum.

1. The name of the company is   J & J Industries Ltd.

2. The authorized capital of the company consists of

    Ten thousand (10 000) Common shares without par value

3. _____We_____ agree to take the number and kind of shares in the company set opposite _____our_____ name.

Full Name(s), Resident Address(es) and Occupation(s) of Subscriber(s)	Number and Kind of Shares taken by Subscriber(s)

John Doe (signature)

John Doe
Teacher
111 A Street
Anywhere, B.C.
Z1P 0G0

Fifty Common shares
without par value

Jack Doe (signature)

Jack Doe
Computer consultant*
222 B Street
Anywhere, B.C.
Z1P 0G0

Fifty Common shares
without par value

Total Shares Taken:

One hundred Common shares
without par value

Dated the _____15th_____ day of _____May_____ , 19 _9-_____

* If you are self-employed, you must specify the nature of your work.

25

FORM 2
(Section 5)

COMPANY ACT

MEMORANDUM

I/We wish to be formed into a specially limited company under the Company Act in pursuance of this Memorandum.

See section 16 (Company Act). It requires these words or their initials after the name.

1. The name of the company is J & J EXPLORATIONS LTD. (Non-Personal Liability).

Paragraph 2 may not be added to, but deletions are permitted.

2. The business that the company is permitted to carry on are restricted to the following:

    (a) exploring for, developing, mining, smelting, milling, and refining materials and coal;

    (b) exploring for, developing, and producing petroleum and natural gas.

Paragraph 3 may be added to, but deletions are not permitted.

3. The company is restricted from exercising the following powers:

    (a) to lend money or to guarantee the contract of any person or corporation, wheresoever incorporated;

    (b) to raise or assist in raising money for, or to aid by way of bonus, promise, endorsement, guarantee of debentures or other securities or otherwise, any person or corporation, wheresoever incorporated.

If you have both par and no par value shares, refer to section 19(3) for description, otherwise omit the reference to the kind of shares you do not have.

4. The authorized capital of the company consists of 3 000 000 to 5 000 000 shares divided into _____ shares with a par value of _____ each and _____ shares without par value.

Any additional provisions here.

5. I/We agree to take the number (and kind) (and class) of shares in the company set opposite my/our name(s).

FULL NAMES, RESIDENT ADDRESSES, CITIZENSHIP AND OCCUPATION OF SUBSCRIBERS	NUMBER (AND KIND) (AND CLASS) OF SHARES TAKEN BY SUBSCRIBERS
John Doe	
John Doe, Teacher 111 A Street Anywhere, B.C. Z1P 0G0 Prospector (Canadian)	Fifty (50) common shares without par value
Jack Doe	
Jack Doe, Businessman 222 B Street Anywhere, B.C. Z1P 0G0 Prospector (Canadian)	Fifty (50) common shares without par value

Total shares taken: One Hundred (100) common shares without par value

DATED the _____15th_____ day of _____May_____ 198-

Note: The provisions of the memorandum may be altered only to the extent and in the manner provided by part 8 of the Company Act.

the First Schedule to the Company Act, you may wish to consider using this set.

Do not adopt the articles as set forth in the Company Act, Table A, unless you have consulted one of the Incorporation Examiners at the Registrar of Companies in Victoria (387-7848). If you decide to adopt the Table A articles, state this on a separate sheet attached to your memorandum, and include your company name and your name and address. This sheet must be signed and dated by you. **Do not** merely state in your covering letter that your company is adopting the articles outlined in the Company Act, Table A; your documents will be rejected by the Registrar. If you adopt your own articles, you must attach two copies when filing your documents. **Note:** The signatures on both sets of articles must be originals, not photocopies. Every non-reporting company must include and comply with provisions in its articles which restrict the transfer of shares and memberships and prohibit soliciting the public to purchase shares. These restrictions are contained in Article 24 of the sample articles.

If you fail to include or comply with these provisions, the Securities Commission will consider your company to be a reporting company and prosecute and fine you for failing to comply with the provisions for reporting companies.

Understand that almost any restriction on share transfer will satisfy the Securities Commission. In the sample articles, the transfer is required to be approved by the directors. (You may, if you prefer, require all transfers to be approved by shareholders.) Article 24 provides the mechanics for obtaining the directors' approval of the share transfer. The selling shareholder must first offer his or her shares to the other shareholders before offering them to any strangers. The existing shareholders have a right to purchase the shares on a "pro rata basis" in order to protect their percentage position in the company.

Pro rata means that the percentage of the shares up for sale that may be purchased by each shareholder is determined by the proportion that each of the remaining shareholders' holdings bears in relation to all of the remaining shareholders' holdings.

For example, in the Rimarri Cookie Company, Mary holds 100 shares, Rick holds 60 shares, and Rita holds 40 shares, and these three are the only shareholders. Mary decides to sell her shares. Since Rick holds 60% of the remaining shares, he could purchase 60% of Mary's shares, or 60 shares. Rita, whose 40 shares represent 40% of the remaining shares, could purchase 40% of the shares for sale, or 40 shares.

No matter what restrictions you adopt, be sure to include them in your articles. To submit your memorandum and articles, make one original and one copy. Two sets of articles are enclosed in the package kit available from the publisher of this book. Be sure to type your company name on the fifth page under the heading "COMPANY ACT" ARTICLES OF. Have the people who signed the memorandum sign the articles in the same manner as they signed the bottom of the memorandum.

Staple the original of your memorandum to the original set of articles and staple the copy of your memorandum to the copy of your articles so that you have two separate, complete sets, each containing a memorandum and a set of articles.

Note: On the articles you submit to the Registrar, do *not* fill in the sample proxy in Article 11.11.

f. DRAFT THE NOTICE OF REGISTERED AND RECORDS OFFICES

The Company Act requires that all businesses incorporated within British Columbia have *two* offices within the province. They are a registered office where legal documents may be served upon the company, and a records office where specific

SAMPLE #7
ARTICLES OF INCORPORATION

ARTICLES
TABLE OF CONTENTS

"COMPANY ACT"
ARTICLES OF

J & J Industries Ltd.

PART 1 — INTERPRETATION

1.1

In these Articles, unless the context otherwise requires:

(a) "Board of Directors" or "Board" means the directors of the Company for the time being;

(b) "casual vacancy" shall mean any vacancy occurring in the Board of Directors of the Company save and except for a vacancy occurring at an annual general meeting of the Company;

(c) "Company Act" means the Company Act of the Province of British Columbia from time to time in force and all amendments thereto and includes all regulations and amendments thereto made pursuant to that Act;

(d) "directors" means the directors of the Company for the time being;

(e) "month" means calendar month;

(f) "ordinary resolution" has the meaning assigned thereto by the Company Act;

(g) "register" means the register of members to be kept pursuant to the Company Act;

(h) "registered address" of a member shall be his address as recorded in the register;

(i) "registered address" of a director means his address as recorded in the Company's register of directors to be kept pursuant to the Company Act;

(j) "reporting company" has the meaning assigned thereto by the Company Act;

(k) "seal" means the common seal of the Company, if the Company has one;

(l) "special resolution" has the meaning assigned thereto by the Company Act.

1.2

Expressions referring to writing shall be construed as including references to printing, lithography, typewriting, photography and other modes of representing or reproducing words in a visible form.

1.3

Words importing the singular include the plural and vice versa; and words importing a male person include a female person and a corporation.

1.4

The definitions in the Company Act shall, with the necessary changes and so far as applicable, apply to these Articles.

1.5

The regulations contained in Table A in the First Schedule to the Company Act shall not apply to the Company.

PART 2 — SHARES AND SHARE CERTIFICATES

2.1

The authorized capital of the Company shall consist of shares of a class or classes, which may be divided into one or more series, as described in the Memorandum of the Company and shall be evidenced or represented in the form of a certificate, and each class of shares shall have a distinct form of certificate.

2.2

Every share certificate issued by the Company shall be in such form as the directors approve and shall comply with the Company Act.

2.3

Every member is entitled, without charge, to one certificate representing the share or shares of each class held by him or upon paying a sum not exceeding the amount permitted by the Company Act, as the directors may from time to time determine, several certificates each for one or more of those shares; provided that, in respect of a share or shares held jointly by several persons, the Company shall not be bound to issue more than one certificate, and delivery of a certificate for a share to one of several joint holders or to his duly authorized agent shall be sufficient delivery to all; and provided further that the Company shall not be bound to issue certificates representing redeemable shares, if such shares are to be redeemed within one month of the date on which they were allotted. Any share certificate may be sent through the post by registered pre-paid mail to the member entitled thereto at his registered address, and the Company shall not be liable for any loss occasioned to the member owing to any such share certificate so sent being lost in the post or stolen.

2.4

Certificates shall be available for delivery by the Company within one month after the allotment of and payment in full for any of its shares, or within one month after the delivery to the Company of an instrument of transfer, unless the conditions of the share otherwise provide, or where the Company has issued shares with a special right to convert attached thereto, within one month after receipt by the Company of the share certificate for the share to be converted properly tendered for conversion.

2.5

If a share certificate:

    (a) is worn out or defaced, the directors may, upon production to them of that certificate and upon such other terms if any, as they may think fit, order the certificate to be cancelled and may issue a new certificate in lieu thereof;

    (b) is lost, stolen or destroyed, then upon proof thereof to the satisfaction of the directors and upon such indemnity, if any, as the directors deem adequate being given, a new share certificate in place thereof shall be issued to the person entitled to the lost, stolen or destroyed certificate, or

    (c) represents more than one share and the registered owner thereof surrenders it to the Company with a written request that the Company issue registered in his name two or more certificates each representing a specified number of shares and in the aggregate representing the same number of shares as the certificate so surrendered, the Company shall cancel the certificate so surrendered and issue in place thereof certificates in accordance with the request.

A sum, not exceeding that permitted by the Company Act, as the directors may from time to time fix, shall be paid to the Company for each certificate issued under this Article.

2.6

Except as required by law or statute or these Articles, no person shall be recognized by the Company as holding any share upon any trust, and the Company shall not be bound by or compelled in any way to recognize (even when having notice thereof) any equitable, contingent, future or partial interest in any share or any interest in any fractional part of a share or (except only as by law or statute or these Articles provided or as ordered by a court of competent jurisdiction) any other rights in respect of any share except an absolute right to the entirety thereof in the registered holder.

2.7

Every share certificate shall be signed manually by at least one officer or director of the Company, or by or on behalf of a registrar, branch registrar, transfer agent or branch transfer agent of the Company and any additional signatures may be printed or otherwise mechanically reproduced and a certificate signed in either of those fashions shall be as valid as if signed manually, notwithstanding that any person whose signature is so printed or mechanically reproduced on a share certificate has ceased to hold the office that he is stated on such certificate to hold at the date of the issue of a share certificate.

2.8

The certificates of shares registered in the name of two or more persons shall be delivered to the person first named on the register.

PART 3 — ISSUE OF SHARES

3.1

The Company may commence business forthwith upon its incorporation notwithstanding that any part of the capital of the Company may remain unallotted or unsubscribed.

3.2

Subject to the Company Act and any provision contained in a resolution passed at a general meeting authorizing any alteration of the capital of the Company, the unissued shares of the Company together with any shares of the Company purchased or redeemed by the Company and not cancelled shall be under the control of the directors who may, subject to the rights of the holders of the shares of the Company for the time being, issue, allot, sell, grant options on, or otherwise dispose of such shares to such persons, including directors, and upon such terms and conditions, and at such price or for such consideration, as the directors, in their absolute discretion, may determine.

3.3

While the Company is not a reporting company and if the directors are so required by the Company Act, they shall, before allotting any shares of the Company, first offer such shares pro rata to the members in the following manner:

   (a) if the shares are not divided into classes the directors shall make such offer pro rata to the members;

   (b) if there are classes of shares, the directors shall make such offer pro rata to the members holding all shares of the class proposed to be allotted and if any shares remain, the directors shall then offer the remaining shares pro rata to the other members;

   (c) any such offer shall be made by notice specifying the number of shares offered and limiting a time for acceptance which shall not be less than seven days;

   (d) after the expiration of the time for acceptance or on receipt of written confirmation from the person to whom the offer is made that he declines to accept the offer, and if there are no other members holding shares who should first receive an offer, the directors may for three months thereafter offer the shares to such persons and in such manner as they think most beneficial to the Company; but the offer to those persons shall not be at a price less than, or on terms more favorable than, the offer to the members; and

   (e) the directors shall not be required to make such an offer to a member who has waived in writing his right to receive such offer and, while the Company is a reporting company, such pro rata offering need not be made.

3.4

The Company may at any time, subject to the Company Act, pay a commission or allow a discount to any person in consideration of his subscribing or agreeing to subscribe, or procuring or agreeing to procure subscriptions, whether absolutely or conditionally, for any shares of the Company, which commission or discount, except where the Company is a specially limited company, shall not, in the aggregate exceed twenty-five percent (25%) of the subscription price. Where the Company is a specially limited company, such discount or commission shall not exceed ninety-five percent (95%) of the subscription price or the par value, whichever is the greater. The company may also pay such brokerage as may be lawful.

3.5

The Company may pay such brokerage fee or other consideration as may be lawful for or in connection with the sale or placement of its securities.

3.6

Except as provided for by the Company Act, no share may be issued until it is fully paid by the receipt by the Company of the full consideration therefor in cash, property or past services actually performed for the Company. The document evidencing indebtedness of the person to whom the shares are allotted is not property for the purpose of this Article. The value of property and services for the purpose of this Article shall be the fair market value thereof as determined by the directors by resolution.

3.7

The directors may determine the price or consideration at or for which shares without par value may be issued.

3.8

The Company may, subject to the Company Act, issue share purchase warrants upon such terms and conditions as the directors shall determine, which share purchase warrants may be issued alone or in conjunction with debentures, debenture stock, bonds, shares or any other security issued or created by the Company from time to time.

PART 4 — SHARE TRANSFERS

4.1

Subject to the restrictions, if any, set forth in these Articles, (see Part 24), any member may transfer his shares by instrument in writing executed by or on behalf of such member and delivered to the Company or its transfer agent. The instrument of transfer of any share of the Company shall be in the form, if any, on the back of the Company's form of share certificates, and in any form which the directors may approve. If the directors so require, each instrument of transfer shall be in respect of only one class of share.

4.2

Every instrument of transfer shall be executed by the transferor and left at the registered office of the Company or at the office of its transfer agent or registrar for registration together with the share certificate for the shares to be transferred and such other evidence, if any, as the directors or the transfer agent or registrar may require to prove the title of the transferor or his right to transfer the shares. All instruments of transfer where the transfer is registered shall be retained by the Company or its transfer agent or registrar and any instrument of transfer, where the transfer is not registered, shall be returned to the person depositing the same together with the share certificate which accompanied the same when tendered for registration. The transferor shall remain the holder of the share until the name of the transferee is entered on the register in respect of that share.

4.3

The signature of the registered owner of any shares, or of his duly authorized attorney, upon the instrument of transfer constitutes an authority to the Company to register the shares specified in the instrument of transfer in the name of the person named in that instrument of transfer as transferee or, if no person is so named, then in any name designated in writing by the person depositing the share certificate and the instrument of transfer with the Company or its agents.

4.4

The Company, and its directors, officers and agents are not bound to enquire into any title of the transferee of any shares to be transferred, and are not liable to the registered or any intermediate owner of those shares, for registering the transfer.

4.5

There shall be paid to the Company in respect of the registration of any transfer a sum, not exceeding that permitted by the Company Act, as the Directors deem fit.

4.6

The Company may appoint one or more trust Companies as its transfer agent or registrar for the purpose of issuing, countersigning, registering, transferring and certifying the shares and share certificates of the Company and the Company may cause to be kept one or more branch registers of members at such places within or without British Columbia. The directors may from time to time by resolution, regulations or otherwise make such provisions as they think fit respecting the keeping of such registers or branch registers.

PART 5 — TRANSMISSION OF SHARES

5.1

In case of the death of a member, not being one of several joint holders, the representative as set out in the Company Act of the deceased shall be the only person recognized by the Company as having any title to the shares registered in the name of such member, and in the case of death of any one or more of the joint registered holders of any share, the survivor or survivors shall be the only person or persons recognized by the Company as having any title to or interest in such share, but nothing herein contained shall release the estate of a deceased joint holder from any liability in respect of any share that had been jointly held by him with other persons.

5.2

A member's guardian, committee, trustee, curator, tutor, personal representative or Trustee in bankruptcy who becomes entitled to a share as a result of the death or bankruptcy of any member shall, upon production to the registered office of the Company of such documents as may be required by the Company Act be registered as holder of the share to which he is so entitled.

5.3

Any person who becomes entitled to a share by operation of statute or as a result of an order of a court of competent jurisdiction, shall, upon production of such evidence as is required by the Company Act, be registered as holder of such share.

PART 6 — ALTERATION OF CAPITAL

6.1

The Company may, by ordinary resolution filed with the Registrar, amend its memorandum to increase the share capital of the Company by:

(a) creating shares with par value or shares without par value, or both;

(b) increasing the number of shares with par value or shares without par value, or both;

(c) increasing the par value of a class of shares with par value, if no shares of that class are issued.

6.2

The directors may, by resolution, increase the consideration at or for which shares without nominal or par value may be issued.

6.3

Except as otherwise provided by conditions imposed at the time of creation of any new shares or by these Articles, any addition to the authorized capital resulting from the creation of new shares shall be subject to the provisions of these Articles.

6.4

Unless these Articles elsewhere specifically otherwise provide, the provisions of these Articles relating to general meetings shall apply, with the necessary changes and so far as they are applicable, to a class meeting of members holding a particular class of shares. A quorum for a class meeting of members shall be one person holding shares of that class present in person at the commencement of the meeting and representing in person or by proxy not less than one-third of the class of shares affected, and one person, if he is a quorum, may constitute a class meeting.

PART 7 — PURCHASE OF SHARES

7.1

Subject to the special rights and restrictions attached to any class of shares, the Company may, by a resolution of the directors and in compliance with the Company Act, purchase any of its shares at the price and upon the terms specified in such resolution or redeem any class or series of its shares in accordance with the special rights and restrictions attaching thereto. No such purchase or redemption shall be made if the Company is insolvent at the time of the proposed purchase or redemption or if the proposed purchase or redemption would render the Company insolvent. Unless the shares are to be purchased through a stock exchange or unless the Company is purchasing the shares from dissenting members pursuant to the requirements of the Company Act, the Company shall make its offer to purchase pro rata to every member who holds shares of the class to be purchased, unless the purchase is of such a nature that the Company Act exempts such purchase from the requirement of making the offer to purchase pro rata to every member who holds shares of the class or series to be purchased.

7.2

If the company proposes at its option to redeem some but not all of the shares of any class or series, the directors may, subject to the special rights and restrictions attached to such class or series, decide the manner in which the shares to be redeemed shall be selected.

7.3

Subject to the provisions of the Company Act, any shares purchased or redeemed by the Company may be sold or issued by it, but, while such shares are held by the Company, it shall not exercise any vote in respect of these shares and no dividend shall be paid thereon.

PART 8 — BORROWING POWERS

8.1

The directors may from time to time at their discretion authorize the Company to borrow any sum of money for the purposes of the Company and may raise or secure the repayment of that sum in such manner and upon such terms and conditions, in all respects, as they think fit, and in particular, and without limiting the generality of the foregoing, by the issue of bonds or debentures, or any mortgage or charge, whether specific or floating, or other security on the undertaking or the whole or any part of the property of the Company, both present and future.

8.2

The directors may make any debentures, bonds or other debt obligations issued by the Company by their terms, assignable free from any equities between the Company and the person to whom they may be issued, or any other person who lawfully acquires the same by assignment, purchase, or otherwise, howsoever.

8.3

The directors may authorize the issue of any debentures, bonds or other debt obligations of the Company at a discount, premium or otherwise, and with special or other rights or privileges as to redemption, surrender, drawings, allotment of or conversion into or exchange for shares, attending at general meetings of the Company and otherwise as the directors may determine at or before the time of issue.

8.4

The Company shall keep or cause to be kept in accordance with the Company Act

    (a) a register of its debentures and debt obligations, and

    (b) a register of the holders of its bonds, debentures and other debt obligations,

and subject to the provisions, the Company Act may keep or cause to be kept one or more branch registers of the holders of its bonds, debentures, or other debt obligations within or without the Province of British Columbia as the directors may from time to time determine and the directors may by resolution, regulations or otherwise make such provisions as they think fit respecting the keeping of such branch registers.

8.5

If the directors so authorize, or if any instrument under which any bonds, debentures or other debt obligations of the Company are issued so provides, any bonds, debentures and other debt obligations of the Company, instead of being manually signed by the directors or officers authorized in that behalf, may have the facsimile signatures of such directors or officers printed or otherwise mechanically reproduced thereon and in either case, shall be as valid as if signed manually, but no such bond, debenture or other debt obligation shall be issued unless it is manually signed, counter-signed or certified by or on behalf of a trust company or other transfer agent or registrar duly authorized by the directors or the instrument under which such bonds, debentures or other debt obligations are issued so to do. Notwithstanding that any persons whose facsimile signature is so used shall have ceased to hold the office that he is stated on such bond, debenture or other debt obligation to hold at the date of the actual issue thereof, the bond, debenture or other debt obligation shall be valid and binding on the Company.

8.6

Unless the conditions of issue of a debenture otherwise provide, the Company shall, within one month after the allotment of and payment for any debenture, have available for delivery the debenture so allotted and paid for. The Company shall, within one month after the delivery to it of an instrument of transfer of a debenture, have available for delivery the debenture transferred. If the directors of the Company refuse to register a transfer of a debenture, a notice of such refusal shall be sent to the prospective transferee within one month after the date on which the instrument of transfer was delivered to the Company.

PART 9 — GENERAL MEETINGS

9.1

Subject to Article 9.2 and to the Company Act, the first annual general meeting shall be held within 15 months from the date of incorporation and thereafter an annual general meeting shall be held once in every calendar year at such time, not being more than 13 months after the holding of the past preceding annual general meeting, and place as the directors shall appoint. In default of the meeting being so held, the meeting shall be held in the month next following and may be called by any two members in the same manner as nearly as possible as that in which meetings are to be called by the directors.

9.2

If the Company is not a reporting company and if all members entitled to attend and vote at the annual general meeting of the Company consent in writing each year to the business required to be transacted at the annual general meeting, that business shall be as valid as if transacted at an annual general meeting duly convened and held and, it is not necessary for the Company to hold an annual general meeting that year.

9.3

Every general meeting, other than an annual general meeting, shall be called an extraordinary general meeting.

9.4

The directors may, whenever they think fit, and they shall, promptly on the receipt of a requisition of a member or members of the Company representing not less than one-twentieth of such of the issued shares in the capital of the Company as at the date of the requisition carry the right of voting in all circumstances at general meetings, call an extraordinary general meeting of the Company.

9.5

Any such requisition, and the meeting to be called pursuant thereto, shall comply with the provisions of the Company Act.

9.6

Not less than 21 days' notice of any general meeting specifying the time and place of meeting and in case of special business, the general nature of that business shall be given in the manner mentioned in Article 21, or in such other manner, if any, as may be prescribed by ordinary resolution whether previous notice thereof has been given or not, to any person as may by law or under these Articles or other regulations of the Company entitled to receive such notice from the Company. But the accidental omission to give notice of any meeting to, or the non-receipt of any such notice by, any of such persons shall not invalidate any proceedings at that meeting.

9.7

All the members of the Company entitled to attend at a general meeting may, by unanimous consent in writing given before, during or after the meeting, or, if they are present at the meeting by a unanimous vote, waive or reduce the period of notice of such meeting, and an entry in the minute book of such waiver or reduction shall be sufficient evidence of the due convening of the meeting. The directors may, for the purpose of determining members entitled to notice of, or to vote at, any general meeting or class meeting fix in advance a date as the record date, which date shall not be more than 49 days before the date of the meeting. Where no such record date is fixed, it shall be deemed to be the date on which the notice calling the general meeting or class meeting is mailed for the purpose of determining those members entitled to notice and to vote at such meeting.

9.8

Where any special business includes the presenting, considering, approving, ratifying or authorizing of the execution of any document, then the portion of any notice relating to such document shall be sufficient if the same states that a copy of the document or proposed document is or will be available for inspection by members at a place in the Province of British Columbia specified in such notice during business hours in any specified working day or days prior to the date of the meeting.

PART 10 — PROCEEDINGS AT GENERAL MEETINGS

10.1

The following business at a general meeting shall be deemed to be special business:

(a) all business at an extraordinary general meeting, and

(b) all business that is transacted at an annual general meeting, with the exception of the consideration of the financial statement and the report of the directors and auditors, the election of directors, the appointment of the auditors and such other business as, under these Articles, ought to be transacted at an annual general meeting, or any business which is brought under consideration by the report of the directors.

10.2

Save as otherwise herein provided a quorum for a general meeting shall be:

(a) two members or proxyholders representing two members; or

(b) one member and a proxyholder representing another member

personally present at the commencement of the meeting and holding or representing by proxy not less than one-twentieth of the issued shares of a class of shares the holders of which are entitled to attend and to vote at such meeting. Where the Company has only one member, the quorum shall be that member or his proxyholder.

10.3

No business, other than the election of a chairman and the adjournment of the meeting shall be transacted at any general meeting unless the quorum requisite is present at the commencement of the meeting, but such quorum need not be present throughout the meeting.

10.4

If within one-half hour from the time appointed for a meeting, a quorum is not present, the meeting, if convened by requisition of the members, shall be dissolved; but in any other case it shall stand adjourned to the same day in the next week at the same time and place. If at such adjourned meeting a quorum is not present within one-half hour from the time appointed, the person or persons present and being or representing by proxy, a member or members entitled to attend and vote at the meeting shall constitute a quorum.

10.5

The Chairman of the Board, if any, or in his absence the President of the Company shall be entitled to preside as chairman at every general meeting of the Company.

10.6

If at any meeting neither the Chairman of the Board, if any, nor the President is present within fifteen minutes after the time appointed for holding the meeting or is willing to act as chairman, the directors present shall choose some one of their number to be chairman. If no director be present or if all the directors present decline to take the chair or shall fail to so choose, the members present shall choose one of their number to be chairman.

10.7

The chairman of the meeting may, with the consent of any meeting at which a quorum is present and shall if so directed by the meeting, adjourn the meeting from time to time and from place to place, but no business shall be transacted at any adjourned meeting other than the business left unfinished at the meeting from which the adjournment took place. When a meeting is adjourned for 30 days or more, notice of the adjourned meeting shall be given as in the case of a general meeting. Save as aforesaid, it shall not be necessary to give any notice of an adjournment or of the business to be transacted at an adjourned meeting.

10.8

Subject to the provisions of the Company Act, every question submitted to a general meeting shall be decided on a show of hands unless a poll is, before or on the declaration of the result of the show of hands, directed by the chairman or demanded by a member entitled to vote who is present in person or by proxy, and the chairman shall declare to the meeting the decision on every question in accordance with the result of the show of hands or the poll, and such decision shall be entered in the book of proceedings of the Company. A declaration by the chairman that a resolution has been carried or carried unanimously or by a particular majority, or lost or not carried by a particular majority, and an entry to that effect in the book containing the minutes of the proceedings of the Company shall be conclusive evidence of the fact without proof of the number or proportion of the votes recorded in favour of or against such resolution.

10.9

No resolution proposed at a meeting need be seconded and the chairman of any meeting shall be entitled to move or second a resolution.

10.10

In case of an equality of votes upon a resolution the chairman shall *not,* either on a show of hands or on a poll, have a casting or second vote in addition to the vote or votes to which he may be entitled as a member.

10.11

Subject to the provisions of Article 10.13, if a poll is duly demanded as aforesaid, it shall be taken in such manner and at such time within seven days from the date of the meeting and place as the chairman of the meeting directs, and either at once or after an interval or adjournment not exceeding seven days, and the result of the poll shall be deemed to be the resolution of the meeting at which the poll is demanded. A demand for a poll may be withdrawn. In the case of any dispute as to the admission or rejection of a vote, the chairman shall determine the same and such determination made in good faith shall be final and conclusive.

10.12

A member entitled to more than one vote need not, if he votes, use all his votes or cast all the votes he uses in the same way.

10.13

No poll may be demanded on the election of a chairman of a meeting and a poll demanded on a question of adjournment shall be taken at the meeting without adjournment.

10.14

The demand of a poll shall not prevent the continuance of a meeting for the transaction of any business other than the question on which a poll has been demanded.

10.15

Every ballot cast upon a poll and every proxy appointing a proxyholder who cast a ballot upon a poll shall be retained by the Secretary for the period and be subject to the inspection as the Company Act may provide.

PART 11 — VOTES OF MEMBERS

11.1

Subject to any special rights or restrictions for the time being attached to any shares, on a show of hands every member present in person shall have one vote, and on a poll every member, present in person or by proxy, shall have one vote for each share which is registered in his name.

11.2

Any person who is not registered as a member but is entitled to vote at any general meeting in respect of a share, may vote the share in the same manner as if he were a member; but, unless the directors have previously admitted his right to vote at that meeting in respect of the share, he shall satisfy the directors of his right to vote the share before the time for holding the meeting, or adjourned meeting, as the case may be, at which he proposes to vote.

11.3

Where there are joint members registered in respect of any share, any one of the joint members may vote at any meeting, either personally or by proxy, in respect of the share as if he were solely entitled to it. If more than one of the joint members is present at any meeting, personally or by proxy, the joint member present whose name stands first on the register in respect of the share shall alone be entitled to vote in respect of that share. Several executors or administrators of a deceased member in whose sole name any share stands shall, for the purpose of this Article, be deemed joint members.

11.4

A corporation, not being a subsidiary of the Company, that is a member may vote by its proxyholder or by its duly authorized representative. Such proxyholder or duly authorized representative is entitled to speak, vote, and in all other respects exercise the rights of a member and shall be deemed to be a member for all purposes in connection with any general meeting of the Company. Where the member is a subsidiary of the Company, the member shall not form part of the quorum, or vote or permit to be voted any shares of the Company registered in its name at a general meeting of members of the Company.

11.5

A member for whom a committee has been duly appointed may vote, whether on a show of hands or on a poll, by his committee and his committee may appoint a proxyholder.

11.6

A member holding more than one share in respect of which he is entitled to vote shall be entitled to appoint one or more proxyholders to attend, act and vote for him on the same occasion. If such a member should appoint more than one proxyholder for the same occasion, he shall specify the number of shares each proxyholder shall be entitled to vote.

11.7

A proxy or an instrument appointing a duly authorized representative of a corporation shall be in writing, under the hand of the appointor or of his attorney duly authorized in writing, or, if such appointor is a corporation, either under its seal or under the hand of an officer or attorney duly authorized.

11.8

A proxyholder need not be a member of the Company if:

(a) the Company is at the time a reporting company, or

(b) the member appointing the proxyholder is a corporation, or

(c) the Company shall have at the time only one member, or

(d) the persons present in person or by proxy and entitled to vote at the meeting by resolution permit the proxyholder to attend and vote; for the purpose of such resolution the proxyholder shall be counted in the quorum but shall not be entitled to vote,

and in all other cases a proxyholder must be a member of the Company.

11.9

A proxy and the power of attorney or other authority, if any, under which it is signed or a notarially certified copy thereof shall be deposited at the registered office of the Company or at such other place as is specified for that purpose in the notice calling the meeting, not less than 48 hours before the time for holding the meeting at which the person named in the proxy proposes to vote, or shall be deposited with the chairman of the meeting prior to the commencement thereof. In addition to any other method of depositing proxies provided for in these Articles, the directors may from time to time make regulations permitting the lodgings of proxies appointing proxyholders at some place or places other than the place at which a meeting or adjourned meeting of members is to be held and for particulars of such proxies to be cabled or telegraphed or sent in writing before the meeting or adjourned meeting to the Company or any agent of the Company for the purpose of receiving such particulars and providing that proxies appointing a proxyholder so lodged may be voted upon as though the proxies themselves were produced to the chairman of the meeting or adjourned meeting as required by this part and votes given in accordance with such regulations shall be valid and shall be counted.

11.10

A vote given in accordance with the terms of a proxy shall be valid notwithstanding the previous death or insanity of the member or revocation of the proxy or of the authority under which the proxy was executed, or the transfer of the share in respect of which the proxy is given, provided no prior notice in writing of the death, insanity, revocation or transfer as aforesaid shall have been received at the registered office of the Company or by the chairman of the meeting or adjourned meeting at which the vote was given.

11.11

Unless, in the circumstances, the Company Act requires any other form of proxy, a proxy appointing a proxyholder, whether for a specified meeting or otherwise, shall be in the form following, or in any other form that the directors shall approve:

(Name of Company)*

The undersigned hereby appoints . . . . (or failing him . . . . of . . . .), as proxyholder for the undersigned to attend at and vote for and on behalf of the undersigned at the general meeting of the Company to be held on the . . . . day of . . . . ,19 . . . . and at any adjournment of that meeting.

Signed this . . . . day of . . . . ,19 . . . .

. . . .

(Signature of Member)

PART 12 — DIRECTORS

12.1

The management of the business of the company shall be vested in the directors and the directors may exercise all such powers and do all such acts and things as the Company is, by its Memorandum or otherwise, authorized to exercise and do, and which are not by these Articles or by statute or otherwise lawfully directed or required to be exercised or done by the Company in general meeting, but subject nevertheless to the provisions of all laws affecting the Company and of these Articles and to any regulations not being inconsistent with these Articles which shall from time to time be made by the Company in general meeting; but no regulation made by the Company in general meeting shall invalidate any prior act of the directors that would have been valid if that regulation had not been made.

*Note: Do not fill in the sample proxy on your copy of these articles.

12.2

The subscriber(s) to the Memorandum are the first directors. The directors to succeed the first directors and the number of directors may be determined in writing by a majority of the subscribers to the Memorandum. The number of directors may be changed from time to time by ordinary resolution, whether previous notice thereof has been given or not, but shall never be less than one while the Company is not a reporting company and three while the Company is a reporting company.

12.3

A director shall not be required to have any share qualification but any person not being a member of the Company who becomes a director shall be deemed to have agreed to be bound by the provisions of the Articles to the same extent as if he were a member of the Company.

12.4

The remuneration of the directors as such may from time to time be determined by the members, unless by ordinary resolution the directors are authorized to determine their remuneration. Such remuneration is to be in addition to any salary or other remuneration paid to any officer or employee of the Company as such, who is also a director. The directors shall be repaid such reasonable expenses as they may incur in and about the business of the Company and if any director shall perform any professional or other services for the Company that in the opinion of the directors are outside the ordinary duties of a director or shall otherwise be specifically occupied in or about the Company's business, he may be paid a remuneration to be fixed by the Board, or, at the option of such director, by the Company in general meeting, and such remuneration may be either in addition to, or in substitution for, any other remuneration that he may be entitled to receive, and the same shall be charged as part of the ordinary working expenses. Unless otherwise determined by ordinary resolution, the directors on behalf of the Company may pay a gratuity or pension or allowance on retirement to any director who has held any salaried office or place of profit with the Company or to his spouse or dependants and may make contributions to any fund and pay premiums for the purchase or provision of any such gratuity, pension or allowance.

12.5

The directors may from time to time and at any time by power of attorney appoint any company, firm or person or body of persons, whether nominated directly or indirectly by the directors, to be the attorney or attorneys of the Company for such purposes and with such powers, authorities and discretions, not exceeding those vested in or exercisable by the directors under these Articles, and for such period and subject to such conditions as they may think fit, and any such powers of attorney may contain such provisions for the protection and convenience of persons dealing with any such attorney as the directors may think fit and may also authorize any such attorney to delegate all or any of the powers, authorities and discretions vested in him.

12.6

A director who is in any way, whether directly or indirectly, interested in a contract or proposed contract or arrangement with the Company shall declare the nature of his interest at a meeting of the directors in accordance with the provisions of the Company Act. A director shall not vote in respect of any such contract or transaction with the Company in which he is interested and if he shall do so his vote shall not be counted, but he may be counted in the quorum present at the meeting at which such vote is taken. Subject to the Company Act, the foregoing shall not apply to

(a) any contract or transaction relating to a loan to the company, which a director or a specified corporation or a specified firm in which he has an interest has guaranteed or joined in guaranteeing the repayment of the loan or any part of the loan, or

(b) any contract or transaction made or to be made with, or for the benefit of an affiliated corporation of which a director is a director or officer, or

(c) determining the remuneration of the directors, or

(d) purchasing and maintaining insurance to cover directors against liability incurred by them as directors, or

(e) the indemnification of any director by the Company.

Subject to the Company Act, the foregoing prohibitions and exceptions thereto may from time to time be suspended or amended to any extent by ordinary resolution, either generally or in respect of any particular contract, arrangement or transaction or for any particular period.

12.7

A director may hold any office or place of profit under the Company, other than auditor, in conjunction with his office of director for such period and on such period and on such terms, as to remuneration or otherwise, as the directors may determine. Subject to compliance with the Company Act, no director or intended director shall be disqualified by his office from contracting with the office or place of profit or as vendor, purchaser or otherwise, and, subject to compliance with the Company Act, no contract or transaction entered into by or on behalf of the Company in which a director is in any way interested shall be liable to be avoided.

12.8

Any director may act by himself or his firm in a professional capacity for the Company, and he or his firm shall be entitled to remuneration for professional services as if he were not a director.

12.9

A director may be or become a director or other officer or employee of, or otherwise interested in, any corporation or firm in which the Company may be interested as a shareholder or otherwise, and, subject to compliance with the provisions of the Company Act, such director shall not be accountable to the Company for any remuneration or other benefits received by him as director, officer or employee of, or from his interest in, such other corporation or firm, unless the Company in general meeting otherwise directs.

12.10

Any director may, from time to time, appoint any person who is approved by resolution of the directors to be his alternate director. The appointee, while he holds office as an alternate director, shall be entitled to notice of meetings of the directors and, in the absence of the director for whom he is an alternate, to attend and vote thereat as a director or sign any resolution of directors to be consented to in writing, and shall not be entitled to be remunerated otherwise than out of the remuneration of the director appointing him. Any director may make or revoke an appointment of his alternate director by notice in writing or by telegram or cable to be delivered or addressed, postage or other charges prepaid, to the registered office of the Company. The directors may by resolution revoke any appointment of an alternate director, any such revocation to become effective upon notice thereof having been given to the director who made the appointment. No person shall act as an alternate for more than one director at any given time and no director may act as an alternate for any other director.

PART 13 — TERMINATION OF DIRECTORSHIP OF DIRECTORS

13.1

The directorship of a director shall be immediately terminated:

(a) if by notice in writing to the Company at its registered office he resigns;

(b) if he is removed pursuant to Article 14.2;

(c) if convicted within or without the Province of an indictable offence and the other directors resolve to remove him; or

(d) if he ceases to be qualified to act as a director under the Company Act.

PART 14 — RETIREMENT AND ELECTION OF DIRECTORS

14.1

At each annual general meeting of the Company all the directors shall retire and the Company shall elect a Board of Directors consisting of the number of directors for the time being fixed pursuant to these Articles. If in any calendar year the Company does not hold an annual general meeting, the directors appointed at the last annual general meeting of the Company shall be deemed to have been elected or appointed as directors on the last day on which the meeting could have been held pursuant to the Company Act and the directors so appointed or elected may hold office until other directors are appointed or elected or until the day on which the next annual general meeting is held.

14.2

The Company may by special resolution remove any director and, by ordinary resolution, appoint another person in his stead. Any director so appointed shall hold office only until the next following annual general meeting of the Company, but shall be eligible for re-election at such meeting.

14.3

The directors shall have power at any time and from time to time to appoint any person as a director, to fill a casual vacancy on the Board or a vacancy resulting from an increase of the number of directors necessitated by the Company Act upon the Company becoming a reporting company. Any director so appointed shall hold office only until the next following annual general meeting of the Company, but shall be eligible for re-election at such meeting.

PART 15 — PROCEEDINGS OF DIRECTORS

15.1

The directors may meet together at such places as they think fit for the dispatch of business, adjourn and otherwise regulate their meetings and proceedings, as they see fit. The directors may from time to time fix the quorum necessary for the transaction of business and unless so fixed such quorum shall be a majority of the Board. The Chairman of the Board, if any, or in his absence the President of the Company, shall be chairman of all meetings of the Board, but if at any meeting neither the Chairman of the Board, if any, nor the President shall be present within 15 minutes after the time appointed for holding the same or if both the Chairman of the Board and the President, being present decline to act, the directors present may choose some one of their number to be chairman at such meeting. A director interested is to be counted in a quorum notwithstanding his interest. In the event the Company is a one-man company, a quorum shall consist of one.

15.2

A director may at any time, and the Secretary shall, upon the written request of a director, call a meeting of the directors. Reasonable notice thereof specifying the time and place of such meeting shall be mailed, postage prepaid, addressed to each of the directors at his registered address before the time fixed for the meeting or such notice may be given to each director either personally or by leaving it at his usual business or residential address or by telephone, telegram, telex or other method of transmitting visually recorded messages. It shall not be necessary to give to any director notice of a meeting of directors immediately following a general meeting at which such director has been elected or notice of a meeting of directors at which such director shall have been appointed. Accidental omission to give notice of a meeting of directors to, or the non-receipt of notice by, any director, shall not invalidate the proceedings at that meeting.

15.3

A meeting of the directors at which a quorum is present shall be competent to exercise all or any of the authorities, power and discretion for the time being vested in or exercisable by the directors.

15.4

The continuing directors may act notwithstanding any vacancy in their body, but, if and so long as their number is reduced below the number fixed pursuant to these Articles as the necessary quorum of directors, the continuing directors or director may act for the purpose of filling vacancies increasing the number of directors to that number, or for the purpose of summoning a general meeting of the Company, but for no other purpose.

15.5

The directors may delegate any but not all of their powers to committees consisting of such of the directors as they think fit. Any committee so formed shall in the exercise of the powers so delegated conform to any regulations that may from time to time be imposed on it by the directors, and shall keep regular minutes of their transactions and shall cause such minutes to be recorded in books kept for that purpose, and shall report the same to the Board of Directors at such times as the Board shall require.

15.6

A committee may elect a chairman of its meetings; if no such chairman is elected, or if at any meetings the chairman is not present within 15 minutes after the time appointed for holding the same, the members present may choose one of their number to be chairman of the meeting.

15.7

The members of a committee may meet and adjourn as they think proper. Questions arising at any meeting shall be determined by a majority of votes of the members present and in case of an equality of votes the chairman shall not have a second or casting vote.

15.8

All acts done by any meeting of the directors or by a committee of directors or by any person acting as a director shall, notwithstanding that it shall be afterwards discovered that there was some defect in the appointment of any such director or person acting as aforesaid, or that they or any of them were disqualified, be as valid as if every such person had been duly appointed and was qualified to be a director.

15.9

For the first meeting of the Board to be held immediately following the appointment or election of a director or directors at an annual or general meeting of shareholders or for a meeting of the Board at which a director is appointed to fill a vacancy in the Board, no notice of such meetings shall be necessary to the newly elected or appointed director or directors in order for the meeting to be duly constituted, provided that a quorum of directors is present.

15.10

Any director of the Company who may be absent either temporarily or permanently from the Province of British Columbia may file at the office of the Company a waiver of notice which may be by letter, telegram or cable of any meeting of the directors and may at any time withdraw such waiver, and until such waiver is withdrawn, no notice of meetings of directors shall be sent to such director, and any and all meetings of the directors of the Company, notice of which shall not have been given to such director, shall, provided a quorum of the directors is present, be valid and binding upon the Company.

15.11

Questions arising at any meeting of the directors shall be decided by a majority of votes. In case of an equality of votes, the Chairman shall not have a second or casting vote.

15.12

A resolution consented to in writing, whether by document, telegram, telex or any method of transmitting legibly recorded messages by all of the directors shall be as valid and effectual as if it had been passed at a meeting of the directors duly called and held. Such resolution may be in two or more counterparts which together shall be deemed to constitute one resolution in writing. Such resolution shall be filed with the minutes of the proceedings of the directors and shall be effective on the dates stated therein or the latest date stated on any counterparts.

15.13

A director may participate in a meeting of the Board or of any committee of the directors through the use of conference telephones or other communication facilities by means of which all directors participating in the meeting can hear each other and provided that all such directors agree to such participation. A director participating in a meeting in accordance with this Article shall be deemed to be present at the meeting and to have so agreed and shall be counted in the quorum therefore and be entitled to speak and vote threat.

PART 16 — OFFICERS

16.1

The Board of Directors shall from time to time appoint a President and a Secretary and may appoint such other officers of the Company as it may determine, none of whom, save the Chairman of the Board, if any, and the President, need be directors. Such officers shall be qualified pursuant to the Company Act to hold office. One person may hold more than one of such offices except that the offices of President and Secretary must be held by different persons unless the Company has only one member.

16.2

All appointments of officers shall be made upon such terms and conditions and at such remuneration, whether by way of salary, fee, commission, participation in profits, or otherwise, as the directors may determine, and every such appointment shall be subject to termination at the pleasure of the directors unless otherwise fixed by contract.

16.3

Every officer of the Company who holds any office or possesses any property whereby, whether directly or indirectly, duties or interests might be created in conflict with his duties or interests as an officer of the Company shall, in writing, disclose to the President the fact and nature, character and extent of the conflict.

16.4

The Secretary of the Company shall:

    (a) keep or cause to be kept the records of the Company in accordance with the provisions of the Company Act;

    (b) make or cause to be made all required filings with the Registrar of Companies for the Province of British Columbia, including the filing within 14 days of being passed, a certified copy of every resolution which by the Company Act does not take effect until such filing has been made; and

    (c) perform such other duties as may be assigned to the office.

PART 17 — MINUTES, DOCUMENTS AND RECORDS

17.1

The directors shall cause minutes to be duly entered in books provided for the purposes:

    (a) of all appointments of officers;

(b) of the names of the directors or their alternates present at each meeting of directors and of any committee of directors;

(c) of all orders made by the directors or committees of directors;

(d) of all resolutions and proceedings of general meetings of the Company and of all meetings of the directors and of committees of directors;

(e) of all waivers signed or resolutions passed by consent being given thereto in writing.

17.2

The directors shall cause the Company to keep at its records office or at such other place as the Company Act may permit, the documents, copy documents, registers, minutes, and records which the Company is required by the Company Act to keep at its records office or such other place.

PART 18 — EXECUTION OF DOCUMENTS

18.1

The directors may provide a common seal for the company and for its use and the directors shall have power from time to time to destroy the same and substitute a new seal in place thereof.

18.2

Subject to the provisions of the Company Act, the directors may provide for use in any other Province, Territory, State or Country an official seal, which shall have on its face the name of the Province, Territory, State or Country where it is to be used.

18.3

If the Company has a common seal, the directors shall provide for its safe custody and it shall not be impressed on any instrument except when such impression is attested by the signature or signatures of:

(a) the President, a Vice-President or director, together with the Secretary or an Assistant Secretary; or

(b) any two directors; or

(c) such one or more directors or officers as may be prescribed from time to time by resolution of the directors; or

(d) where the company has but one director, that director or the Secretary or an Assistant Secretary.

18.4

The signature of any officer of the Company may, if authorized by the directors, be printed, lithographed, engraved or otherwise mechanically reproduced upon all instruments executed or issued by the Company or any officer thereof; and any instrument on which the signature of any such person is so reproduced shall be deemed to have been manually signed by such person whose signature is so reproduced and shall be as valid to all intents and purposes as if such instrument had been signed manually, and notwithstanding that the person whose signature is so reproduced may have ceased to hold office at the date of the delivery or issue of such instrument. The term "instrument" as used in this Article shall include deeds, mortgages, hypothecs, charges, conveyances, transfers and assignments of property, real or personal, agreements releases, receipts and discharges for the payment of money or other obligations, certificates of the Company's shares, share warrants of the Company, bonds, debentures and other debt obligations of the Company, and all paper writings.

PART 19 — DIVIDENDS

19.1

The directors may declare dividends and fix the date of record therefore and the date for payment thereof. No notice need be given of the declaration of any dividend. If no date of record is fixed, the date of record shall be deemed to be the same date as the date the dividend is declared. No dividend shall be paid otherwise than out of funds and/or assets properly available for the payment of dividends and a declaration by the directors as to the sufficiency of such funds and/or assets available for dividends shall be conclusive.

19.2

Subject to the terms of shares with special rights or restrictions, all dividends shall be declared according to the number of shares held.

19.3

No dividend shall bear interest against the Company. Where the dividend to which a member is entitled includes a fraction of a cent, such fraction shall be disregarded in making payment thereof and such payment shall be deemed to be payment in full.

19.4

The directors may direct payment of any dividend wholly or partly by the distribution of specific assets or of paid-up shares, bonds, debentures or other debt obligations of the Company, or in any one or more of these ways, and, where any difficulty arises in regard to the distribution, the directors may settle the same as they think expedient, and in particular may fix the value for distribution of specific assets, and may determine that cash payments shall be made to a member upon the basis of the value so fixed in place of fractional shares, bonds, debentures or other debt obligations in order to adjust the rights of all parties, and may vest any of those specific assets in trustees upon such trusts for the persons entitled as may seem expedient to the directors.

19.5

Notwithstanding anything contained in these Articles, the directors may from time to time capitalize any undistributed surplus on hand of the Company and may from time to time issue as fully paid and non-assessable any unissued shares or any bonds, debentures or other debt obligations of the Company as a dividend representing such undistributed surplus on hand or any part thereof.

19.6

Any dividend, interest or other monies payable in cash in respect of shares may be paid by cheque or warrant sent through the post directed to the registered address of the holder, or, in the case of joint holders, to the registered address of that one of the joint holders who is first named on the register or to such person and to such address as the holder or joint holders may in writing direct. Every such cheque or warrant shall be made payable to the order of the person to whom it is sent. Any one of two or more joint holders may give effectual receipts for any dividends, bonuses or other monies payable in respect of the shares held by them as joint holders, and the Company is not bound to see to the execution of any trust in respect of shares of the Company. The mailing of such cheque or warrant shall, to the extent of the sum represented thereby (plus the amount of any tax required by law to be deducted) discharge all liability for the dividend, unless such cheque or warrant shall not be paid on presentation or the amount of tax so deducted is not paid to the appropriate taxing authority.

19.7

No dividend shall be paid if:

(a) the Company is insolvent; or

(b) the payment of the dividend would render the Company insolvent; or

(c) the Company has outstanding shares containing rights which provide that those shares shall be redeemed or purchased on or before a certain date and provision has not been made for a capital redemption fund in compliance with the Company Act.

19.8

A transfer of a share shall not pass the right to any dividend declared thereon before the registration of the transfer in the register.

19.9

Notwithstanding any other provisions of these Articles should any dividend result in any shareholders being entitled to a fractional part of a share of the Company, the directors shall have the right to pay such shareholders in place of that fractional share, the cash equivalent thereof calculated on the par value thereof or, in the case of shares without nominal or par value, calculated on the price or consideration for which such shares were or were deemed to be issued, and shall have the further right and complete discretion to carry out such distribution and to adjust the rights of the shareholders with respect thereto on as practical and equitable a basis as possible including the right to arrange through a fiscal agent or otherwise for the sale, consolidation or other disposition of those fractional shares on behalf of those shareholders of the Company.

19.10

The directors may, before declaring any dividend, set aside out of the profits of the Company such sums as they think proper as appropriations from income, which shall at the discretion of the directors, be applicable for meeting contingencies, or for equalizing dividends, or for any other purpose to which the profits of the company may be properly applied, and pending such application may, either be employed in the business of the Company or be invested in such investments as the directors in their discretion may from time to time determine.

PART 20 — ACCOUNTS

20.1

The directors shall cause records and books of accounts to be kept as necessary to properly record the financial affairs and conditions of the Company and to comply with the provisions of statutes applicable to the Company.

20.2

The directors shall determine the place at which the accounting records of the Company shall be kept and those records shall be open to the inspection of any director during the normal business hours of the Company.

20.3

The directors shall determine to what extent, at what times and places and under what conditions the accounting records of the Company shall be open to the inspection of members.

PART 21 — NOTICES

21.1

In this Part 21, unless the context otherwise requires, the word notice shall include a notice, statement, report or any other document.

21.2

In addition to any other method of giving notice as set out in the Company Act, or as otherwise set out in these Articles, a notice may be given or delivered to any member or director, either personally or by sending it by post to him in a letter, envelope or wrapper, postage prepaid, addressed to the member or director at his registered address. A certificate signed by the Secretary or other officer of the Company or of any other corporation acting in that behalf for the Company that the letter, envelope or wrapper containing the notice, statement or report was so addressed, prepaid and mailed shall be conclusive evidence thereof.

21.3

A notice may be given by the Company to joint members in respect of a share registered in their names by giving the notice to the joint member first named in the register of members in respect of that share.

21.4

A notice may be given by the Company to the persons entitled to a share in consequence of the death or bankruptcy of a member by sending it through the post in a prepaid letter, envelope or wrapper addressed to them by name, or by the title of representatives of the deceased, or trustee of the bankrupt, or by any like description, at the address, if any, supplied for the purpose by the persons claiming to be so entitled, or until that address has been so supplied, by giving the notice in any manner in which the same might have been given if the death or bankruptcy had not occurred.

21.5

Any notice or document sent by post to or left at the registered address of any member shall, notwithstanding that member is then deceased and whether or not the Company has notice of his death, be deemed to have been duly served in respect of any registered shares, whether held solely or jointly with other persons by that deceased member, until some other person is registered in his place as the member or joint member in respect of those shares, and that service shall for all purposes of these Articles be deemed a sufficient service of such notice or document on his personal representatives and all persons, if any, jointly interested with him in those shares.

21.6

Any notice sent by post shall be deemed to have been served on the day following that on which the letter, envelope or wrapper containing that notice is posted, and in proving service thereof it shall be sufficient to prove that the letter, envelope or wrapper containing the notice was properly addressed and put in a Canadian Government post office, postage prepaid.

21.7

If a number of days' notice or a notice extending over any other period is required to be given, the day of service shall not, unless it is otherwise provided in these Articles, be counted in the number of days or other period required.

21.8

Notice of every general meeting shall be given in the manner authorized by these Articles, to:

    (a) every member holding a share or shares carrying the right to vote at such meetings on the record date or, if no record date was established by the directors, on the date of mailing;

    (b) the personal representative of a deceased member;

    (c) the trustee in bankruptcy of a bankrupt member; and

    (d) the auditor of the Company, if any.

PART 22 — INDEMNIFICATION AND PROTECTION OF DIRECTORS, OFFICERS, EMPLOYEES, AND CERTAIN AGENTS

22.1

The Company shall indemnify any person who was or is a party or is threatened to be made a party to any threatened, pending or completed action or proceeding, whether or not brought by the Company or by a corporation or other legal entity or enterprise, officer, employee, or agent of the Company or is or was serving at the request of the Company as a director, officer, employee or agent of another corporation, a partnership, joint venture, trust or other enterprise, against all costs, charges and expenses, including legal fees and any amount paid to settle the action or proceeding or satisfy a judgment, if he acted honestly and in good faith with a view to the best interests of the corporation or other legal entity or enterprise as aforesaid of which he is or was a director, officer, employee or agent, as the case may be, and exercised the care, diligence and skill of a reasonably prudent person, and with respect to any criminal or administrative action or proceeding, he had reasonable grounds for believing that his conduct was lawful; provided that no one shall be indemnified hereunder:

(a) if he has failed to carry out his duty to act in accordance with the Company Act or any rule of law; and in any event,

(b) until court approval has been granted with respect to such indemnification.

The determination of any action, suit or proceeding by judgment, order, settlement, conviction or otherwise shall not, of itself, create a presumption that the person did not act honestly and in good faith and in the best interests of the Company and did not exercise the care, diligence and skill of a reasonably prudent person and, with respect to any criminal action or proceeding, did not have reasonable grounds to believe that his conduct was lawful.

22.2

The Company shall indemnify any person other than a director in respect of any loss, damage, costs or expenses whatsoever incurred by him while acting as an officer, employee or agent for the Company unless such loss, damage, costs or expenses shall arise out of failure to comply with instructions, wilful act or default or fraud by such person in any of which events the Company shall only indemnify such person if the directors, in their absolute discretion, so decide or the Company by ordinary resolution shall so direct.

22.3

The indemnification provided by this Part shall not be deemed exclusive of any other rights to which those seeking indemnification may be entitled under any other Part, or any valid and lawful agreement, vote of members or disinterested directors or otherwise, both as to action in his official capacity and as to action in another capacity while holding such office, and shall continue as to a person who has ceased to be a director, officer, employee or agent and shall ensure to the benefit of the heirs, executors and administrators of such person. The indemnification provided by this Article shall not be exclusive of any powers, rights, agreements or undertakings which may be legally permissible or authorized by or under any applicable law. Notwithstanding any other provisions set forth in this Part, the indemnification authorized by this Part shall be applicable only to the extent that any such indemnification shall not duplicate indemnity or reimbursement which that person has received or shall receive otherwise than under this Part.

22.4

The directors are authorized from time to time to cause the Company to give indemnities to any director, officer, employee, agent or other person who has undertaken or is about to undertake any liability on behalf of the Company or any corporation controlled by it. The failure of a director or officer of the Company to comply with the provisions of the Company Act, the Memorandum or these Articles shall not invalidate any indemnity to which he is entitled under this Part.

22.5

Subject to the Company Act, no director or officer or employee for the time being of the Company shall be liable for the acts, receipts, neglects or defaults of any other director or officer or employee, or for joining in any receipt or act for conformity, or for any loss, damage or expense happening to the Company through the insufficiency or deficiency of any security in or upon which any of the monies of or belonging to the Company shall be invested or for any loss or damages arising from the bankruptcy, insolvency, or tortious act of any person, firm or corporation with whom or which any monies, securities or effects shall be lodged or deposited or for any loss occasioned by any error of judgment or oversight on his part or for any other loss, damage or misfortune whatever which may happen in the execution of the duties of his respective office or trust or in relation thereto unless the same shall happen by or through his own wilful act or default, negligence, breach of trust or breach of duty.

22.6

Directors may rely upon the accuracy of any statement of fact represented by an officer of the Company to be correct or upon statements in a written report of the auditor of the Company and shall not be responsible or held liable for any loss or damage resulting from the paying of any dividends or otherwise acting in good faith upon any such statement.

22.7

The directors may cause the Company to purchase and maintain insurance for the benefit of any person who is or was a director, officer, employee or agent of the Company or is or was serving at the request of the Company as a director, officer, employee or agent of another corporation, a partnership, joint venture, trust or other enterprise and his heirs and representatives against any liability incurred by him as a director, officer, employee or agent.

PART 23 — PROHIBITIONS

23.1

No transfer of shares shall be entered in the register of members without the prior approval of the majority of directors, and the Company shall not keep a branch register of members outside the Province of British Columbia unless the Company Act so permits.

PART 24 — RESTRICTIONS ON SHARE TRANSFERS

24.1

Notwithstanding anything contained in these Articles the directors may in their absolute discretion decline to register any transfer of shares and shall not be required to disclose their reasons therefor; provided that at such time as the securities of the Company have been listed for trading on any stock exchange or any regulatory authority has accepted for filing and has issued a receipt for a prospectus qualifying the distribution of the Company's securities to the public, any restriction on the transfer of shares of the Company shall, by that fact, be removed.

24.2

No shares in the capital of the Company shall be transferred by any member, or the personal representative of any deceased member or trustee in bankruptcy of any bankrupt member, or the liquidator of a member which is a corporation, except under the following conditions.

(a) A person (herein called the "proposing transferor") desiring to transfer any share or shares in the Company shall give notice in writing (herein called the "transfer notice") to the Company that he desires to transfer the same. The transfer notice shall specify the price, which shall be expressed in lawful money of Canada, and the terms of payment upon which the proposing transferor is prepared to transfer the share or shares and shall constitute the Company his agent for the sale thereof to any member or members of the Company at the price and upon the terms of payment so specified. The transfer notice shall also state whether or not the proposing transferor has had an offer to purchase the shares or any of them from, or proposes to sell the shares or any of them to, any particular person or persons who are not members and if so the names and addresses of such persons shall be specified in the transfer notice. The transfer notice shall constitute an offer by the proposing transferor to the other members of the Company holding shares of the class or classes included in the transfer notice and shall not be revocable except with the sanction of the directors. If the transfer notice pertains to shares of more than one class, then the consideration and terms of payment for each class of shares shall be stated separately in the transfer notice.

(b) The directors shall forthwith upon receipt thereof transmit the transfer notice to each of the members, other than the proposing transferor, holding shares of the class or classes set forth in the transfer notice and request the member to whom the transfer notice is sent to state in writing within 14 days from the date of the transfer notice whether he is willing to accept any, and if so, the maximum number of shares he is willing to accept at the price and upon the terms specified in the transfer notice. A member shall only be entitled to purchase shares of the class or classes held by him.

(c) Upon the expiration of the 14-day notice period referred to in Article 24.2 (b), if the directors shall have received from the members entitled to receive the transfer notice sufficient acceptances to take up the full number of shares offered by the transfer notice and, if the transfer notice includes shares of more than one class, sufficient acceptances from the members of each class to take up the full number of shares of each class offered by the transfer notice, the directors shall thereupon apportion shares so offered among the members so accepting and so far as may be, pro rata, according to the number of shares held by each of them respectively, and in the case of more than one class of shares, then pro rata in respect of each class. If the directors shall not have received sufficient acceptances as aforesaid, they may, but only with the consent of the proposing transferor who shall not be obliged to sell to members in the aggregate less than the total number of shares of one or more classes of shares offered by the transfer notice, apportion the shares so offered among the members so accepting so far as may be according to the number of shares held by each respectively but only up to the amount accepted by such members respectively. Upon any such apportionment being made the proposing transferor shall be bound upon payment of the price to transfer the shares to the respective members to whom the directors have apportioned same. If, in any case, the proposing transferor, having become so bound fails in transferring any share, the Company may receive the purchase money for that share and shall upon receipt cause the name of the purchasing member to be entered in the register as the holder of the shares and cancel the certificate of the share held by the proposed transferor, whether the same shall be produced to the Company or not, and shall hold such purchase money in trust for the proposing transferor. The receipt of the Company for the purchase money shall be a good discharge to the purchasing member and after his name has been entered in the register the validity of the proceedings shall not be questioned by any person.

(d) In the event that some or all of the shares offered shall not be sold under the preceding Articles within the 14 day period referred to in Article 24.2 (b), the proposing transferor shall be at liberty for a period of 90 days after the expiration of that period to transfer such of the shares so offered as are not sold to any person provided that he shall not sell them at a price less than that specified in the transfer notice or on terms more favourable to a purchaser than those specified in the transfer notice.

(e) The provisions as to transfer contained in this Article shall not apply:

(i) if before the proposed transfer of shares is made, the transferor shall obtain consents to the proposed transfer from members of the Company, who at the time of the transfer are the registered holders of two-thirds or more of the issued shares of the class to be transferred of the Company or if the shares comprise more than one class, then from the registered holders of two-thirds or more of the shares of each class to be transferred and such consent shall be taken to be a waiver of the application of the preceding Articles as regards such transfer; or

(ii) to a transfer of shares desired to be made merely for the purpose of effectuating the appointment of a new trustee for the owner thereof, provided that it is proved to the satisfaction of the Board that such is the case.

FULL NAME(S), ADDRESS(ES), AND OCCUPATION(S) OF SUBSCRIBERS

John Doe, Teacher
111 A Street
Anywhere, B.C. Z1P 0G0

John Doe

Jack Doe, Businessman
222 B Street
Anywhere, B.C. Z1P 0G0

Jack Doe

DATED at ___Anywhere, B.C.___, this __15th__ day of __May__, 19_9-_.

registers and documents must be kept ready for inspection by members, employees, creditors, and the general public. Most companies have both offices at the same address.

These provisions are to enable people like minority shareholders and creditors of the company to be well informed. They are also meant to encourage thorough record keeping by all British Columbia companies. There is little proof that this is the actual result of the requirements for a records office, but the penalties for failing to comply with the requirements are severe, so it is imperative that you take steps to comply with the provisions regarding record keeping and rights to inspect that are contained in the Company Act.

If it is a problem for you to keep your own records, you might consider using the "records office" services offered by many lawyers. The annual charge for this service usually ranges from $150 to $300.

The locations of your registered and records office must be places that can be found. The addresses may not be post office box numbers as the Company Act requires that certain documents and registers and the seal (if purchased) of the company be physically kept at the registered and/or records office. In some cases, this may be your primary place of business.

Sample #8 shows a Notice of Offices.

1. What documents are kept at the records office?

The secretary of the company is responsible for filing and keeping at the records office the documents listed in Table #2.

2. Who may see the records?

A person's rights to review the company records depends on his or her relationship to the company (shareholder, creditor, etc.) and whether the company is a reporting or a non-reporting company.

For example, every director may examine and take copies of all the documents listed in section 187 at no charge. A former director has the same privileges with respect to documents relating to the time of his or her directorship.

If you are a member shareholder or debenture holder (i.e., loaned money to the company secured by a debenture), you may look at and copy any document listed in section 187(1) except for items in paragraphs (l), (q), (r) and (t)(ii). (See Table #2.)

For a reporting company, anyone has the same privileges as a shareholder but must pay 50¢ for each document looked at. For a non-reporting company, anyone may look at and copy any document except those in paragraphs (k), (l), (q), (r), (s) and (t)(ii) and (iii) of section 187(1). (See Table #2.) A 50¢ fee per document examined is also charged in this case.

Your records office must be set up so that the listed documents and registers are available for inspection for at least two consecutive business hours per business day. Anyone who is entitled to review the documents is entitled to receive copies for a fee of no more than 50¢ per page.

Your records may be kept in bound or loose-leaf form or by electrical or mechanical data processing. Whatever form you choose, you must be able to reproduce the required information within a reasonable time.

You must set up your records office so that the documents may be promptly reached, and so that they are reasonably protected from loss or destruction and from falsification. This latter requirement necessitates someone being there whenever anyone looks at the company records to ensure that no alterations or false entries are made.

Your records office will probably be the source of the free copy of the memorandum and articles to which every shareholder is entitled. It will also be responsible for preparing a list of shareholders with their names and addresses and the number

FORM 3
(Section 8)

PROVINCE OF BRITISH COLUMBIA

COMPANY ACT

NOTICE OF OFFICES

The offices of the undermentioned Company are located as follows:

Name of Company .... J & J Industries Ltd. ....

....

Registered Office:

Address ... 222 A Street ....
         Anywhere, British Columbia Z1P 0G0
....

British Columbia

Records Office:

Address .... 333 B Street ....
         Anywhere, British Columbia Z1P 0G0
....

British Columbia

Dated the __15th__ day of __May__ , 19 _9-_ .

(Signature) .... *John Doe* ....

(Relationship to Company) ..... Subscriber ....

TABLE #2
DOCUMENTS REQUIRED TO BE KEPT AT RECORDS OFFICE

Records office documents

187. (1) Every company shall keep at its records office
- (a) its certificate of incorporation;
- (b) a copy of its memorandum, including every amendment of it;
- (c) a copy of its articles, including every amendment of it;
- (d) its register of members, except as provided by section 69;
- (e) its register of transfers, unless the register of members is kept elsewhere as provided by section 69;
- (f) its register of directors;
- (g) its register of debentureholders, except as provided by section 88 or 89;
- (h) its register of debentures;
- (i) its register of indebtedness;
- (j) its register of allotment, unless the register of members is kept elsewhere as provided by section 69;
- (k) the minutes of every general meeting and class meeting of the company;
- (l) the minutes of every meeting of its directors;
- (m) a copy of every document filed with the registrar;
- (n) a copy of every certificate issued to it by the registrar;
- (o) a copy of every order of the minister of the registrar relating to the company;
- (p) a copy of every written contract under which the company has allotted any shares for a consideration other than cash;
- (q) a copy of every other document and instrument approved in the preceding 10 years by the directors;
- (r) a copy of every mortgage created or assumed by the company, whether or not required to be registered;
- (s) a copy of every audited financial statement of the company and its subsidiaries, whether or not consolidated with the financial statement of the company, including the auditor's reports;
- (t) where the company is an amalgamated company,
  - (i) every record, document or instrument described in paragraphs (a) to (j), (m) to (p) and (u) to (w);
  - (ii) every record, document or instrument described in paragraphs (l), (q) and (r); and
  - (iii) every record, document or instrument described in paragraphs (k) and (s);
  of each of the amalgamating companies;
- (u) where the company is being wound up, the minutes of every meeting of its creditors;
- (v) a copy of every prospectus and takeover bid circular issued in the preceding 10 years by the company or any subsidiary;
- (w) a copy of every information circular issued in the preceding 10 years by the company or any subsidiary;
- (x) a copy of the instrument of continuation under section 36, if any; and
- (y) where a receiver or receiver-manager is appointed under an instrument registered in the office of the registrar, the name and address of the receiver or receiver-manager, the date of the appointment of the receiver or receiver-manager and either the date he ceases to act or the date of the completion of his duties.

(2) Except as provided in subsection (3), the records, documents and instruments referred to in subsection (1) are those established or made, and the information in them shall relate to matters occurring after October 1, 1973.

(3) The records, documents and instruments referred to in subsection (1)(a) to (d), (g) and (k) of subsection (1) are those relating to matters occurring since the incorporation of the company, or of the amalgamating companies, as the case may be, but, with respect to the period before October 1, 1973, only to the extent that the records, documents or instruments referred to in those paragraphs were required to be kept by the provisions of any former Companies Act.

(4) Every company that contravenes this section commits an offence.

[1973-18-186; 1973-103-6; 1976-12-39; 1987-56-48; 1989-47-306; 1990-11-4].

of shares each holds, or a list of names and addresses of all debenture holders as of a date not more than 14 days before the list is delivered to someone who applies for it. The applicant must make his or her request in writing, and accompany this request with a statutory declaration disclosing the name of the applicant and promising that the list shall be used only for "corporate purposes." This means that the list will be used in an effort to solicit votes of shareholders or debenture holders at a meeting to acquire or sell shares or debentures, to cause the company to amalgamate, or to make some other reorganization. A reasonable fee may be charged by the company for preparing this list.

If you fail to keep the required records or refuse to let a shareholder examine them, you are guilty of an offence and liable to a serious fine. If you authorize or permit any of these offences as a director, you are also guilty of an offence and personally liable for any fines. If you are responsible for the accuracy of the company records, and if a false statement is made in any record, or if an important material fact is left out, then you may be found guilty of an offence and liable to a fine. Company secretaries take note!

g. PROCEDURE FOR FILING DOCUMENTS

Whenever you file any documents, try to arrange for everyone to attend a single signing session, so all forms will have the same date. Be sure all forms have the postal codes of all addresses listed. Mail the two sets of memorandum and articles along with two copies of the Notice of Offices (as shown in Sample #8), the cheque covering your fees for incorporation and for certifying your memorandum and articles (made payable to the Minister of Finance), and your covering letter. A sample covering letter is shown in Sample #9.

The Registrar offers a priority service on processing documents. If you are in a hurry to receive your incorporation papers, you can pay a $100 fee on top of the regular incorporation fees and request priority service in your covering letter.

This covering letter and the letter requesting name search and reservation of name are the only letters required when dealing with the Registrar of Companies in routine matters. For all subsequent filings the documents are accompanied by a "remittance form." These forms are provided free of charge by the Registrar's office in Victoria upon request. The original copy of the form serves as a receipt for fees paid on filing and is returned by the office of the Registrar to the address given on the form when the filing is completed. All cheques sent to the Registrar of Companies must be made payable to the "Minister of Finance."

If your documents are in order, certified copies of your documents will be returned to you along with the Certificate of Incorporation. Allow at least two weeks for your documents to be returned from Victoria. Your certificate will resemble the one in Sample #11.

Remember that if your documents are rejected for any reason by the Registrar, you will have to pay an additional fee when resubmitting your forms, so double-check all your forms for completeness of required information and signatures before submitting them. You should also confirm by telephone the current fees, as fees given in this book may have changed since publication.

The Registrar will also publish a notice of your incorporation in the *British Columbia Gazette* (see Sample #10). The actual notice in the *Gazette* merely lists the company name and incorporation number. However, you will need to know the *Gazette* reference (volume and page numbers) if you intend to purchase, sell, or otherwise deal in real property, mortgages, etc. These particulars will be required by the Land Title Office when the first land transaction is presented for filing.

You may obtain particulars of the *Gazette* notice from the public library or purchase a copy of the *Gazette* containing news of the registration of your company from Crown Publications in Victoria. For the current price of purchasing a copy of the *Gazette*, telephone 386-4636 or contact:

Crown Publications
546 Yates Street
Victoria, B.C.
V8W 1K8

Be sure to note the exact date of incorporation so they can locate the correct issue for you.

SAMPLE #9
LETTER TO REGISTRAR

John Doe
123 East Street
Vancouver, B.C.
V1P 0G0

May 16, 199-

Ministry of Finance and Corporate Relations
Corporate, Central and Mobile Home Registry
940 Blanshard Street
Victoria, B.C.
V8W 3E6

**Re: Incorporation of
J & J Industries Ltd.**

Enclosed are the following documents.

1.   Original and one copy of Memorandum and Articles.

2.   Notice of Offices (Form 3 — original and copy)

3.   Our cheque in the amount of $300*, payable to the Minister of Finance, to cover your fees.

The name J & J Industries Ltd. was reserved with your office under number 45678. Would you kindly attend to the incorporation of the above-mentioned company and return certified copies of the enclosed documents as soon as possible?

Yours truly,

John Doe

John Doe

*Note: This amount will vary depending on your circumstances and whether the fees have changed. Please check with the Registrar for current fees before submitting your documents.

GAZETTE NOTICE
COMPANY ACT

NOTICE is hereby given of the incorporation of the following companies:

December 15, 199-
143587   Sky-Glider Recreations (1986) Ltd.

December 16, 199-
143689   Canwest Publishers Limited

December 17, 199-
143691   Alderwood Projects Ltd.
143724   Alginure Products Canada Ltd.
143705   Amar Developments Ltd.

CANADA
PROVINCE OF BRITISH COLUMBIA

NUMBER

123,456

Province of British Columbia
Ministry of Finance and Corporate Relations
REGISTRAR OF COMPANIES

COMPANY ACT

Certificate of Incorporation

I HEREBY CERTIFY THAT

J & J Industries Ltd.

HAS THIS DAY BEEN INCORPORATED UNDER THE COMPANY ACT

GIVEN UNDER MY HAND AND SEAL OF OFFICE

AT VICTORIA, BRITISH COLUMBIA,

THIS   1st   DAY OF   JUNE , 199-

DEPUTY REGISTRAR OF COMPANIES

5

POST-INCORPORATION PROCEDURES

You have received your certificate from Victoria. What do you do next?

a. PURCHASE MINUTE BOOK, COMPANY SEAL, AND SHARE CERTIFICATES

The Company Act requires that minutes of all company meetings, as well as copies of all the other documents previously listed, be kept at the records office in a minute book maintained for that purpose. Therefore, if you have not yet obtained a minute book, you should do so now. Insert the certified copies of your documents returned to you by the Registrar under the proper tabs in your minute book.

It is mandatory to keep a directors' register as shown in Sample #12 and members' registers (i.e., registers of shareholders, share allotments, and share transfers) as shown in Samples #13, #14, and #15. (**Note:** The registers can be written; they do not need to be typed.)

Strictly speaking, you do not require a company seal any more. However, the Land Title Act has not been changed to reflect this, which means that if you intend to deal in land in any fashion, you must get a seal or face numerous rejected documents. Furthermore, many banks insist upon your "sealing" all agreements that the company makes with the bank. You may politely point out the law and, in some cases, may avoid having the seal by simply signing a letter waiving your company's use of the seal. Nevertheless, you will save yourself a great deal of needless bother if you simply order a seal.

When you need a seal, you may order it from the publisher. (Please refer to page xii for details.) But in any case, you should not order a seal until you receive your Certificate of Incorporation from the Registrar. Any slight deviation from the company's name on the certificate will render the seal virtually useless. (The names must be identical in, for example, land transactions.)

b. BANKING ARRANGEMENTS

Your company, since it is a separate legal entity, must have its own bank account and deposit, withdrawal, and chequing arrangements, etc. These arrangements are determined by resolutions of the company and by agreement with the bank.

You may wish to consider opening an account at a trust company or credit union. Unlike banks, trust companies and credit unions normally pay interest on chequing accounts. However, if you need financing, a bank is probably your best bet because it will lend money on security, like an assignment of accounts receivable, whereas a trust company or credit union advances loans mainly on mortgages, and will not accept other types of security.

Your bank manager will provide the necessary forms (banking resolutions) for you to fill out.

c. POST-INCORPORATION ORGANIZATION

After you have purchased your minute book, decided what bank your company is going to use, etc., you must prepare your organizational consent resolutions.

Although these resolutions do not have to be filed with the Registrar of Companies, it is very important to have them signed and in the minute book. That way, if at a later date, a dissident member or director challenges certain company proceedings, the documents are on file for ready inspection. This happens more often than you may think, and you will leave yourself open for trouble if these resolutions are not prepared and then signed by all parties concerned.

1. Subscribers' resolutions

Your first resolution will be by the subscribers to the memorandum for the purpose of formally approving and adopting the documents of incorporation and incorporating them into the minute book, for electing the directors, and for waiving audit for the first year.

To simplify matters, the resolutions in Sample #16 combine the resolutions of the first directors and the subscribers to the memorandum as is done in many law firms. In this sample, the first few resolutions, down to "Election of Officers," are the subscribers' section, and by reading them you will understand what you are supposed to do.

2. Directors' resolutions

Next comes the preparation of the directors' section. As you can see from Sample #16, the first resolutions of the directors are usually designed to transfer the subscribers' shares to permanent shareholders (if applicable), elect officers, appoint a banker, authorize transfer of assets into the company (again if applicable), and other miscellaneous transactions.

Remember, it is the directors who sit in power and who, theoretically, direct the company on all important issues. When-

ever an important issue arises, it is resolved by the directors and confirmed by resolutions in writing as shown in Sample #16.

3. Consents to act as director

Every director must consent in writing to act as a director unless present at the meeting at which he or she is elected. (See Sample #27.) As most closely held companies pass consent resolutions, a consent to act as director should be signed by every director.

d. USE OF THE COMPANY NAME

In British Columbia, all companies are required to display their names legibly on the outside of all places of business, on contracts, business letters, orders for goods, invoices, statements, receipts, and letters of credit. Promissory notes, bills of exchange, cheques, and money orders must also receive the same treatment if they are made on behalf of the company. (See section 130 of the Company Act.)

Furthermore, an officer who misleads someone by authorizing or issuing a document that does not properly display the company name is personally responsible for making good any loss arising from misleading the recipient.

Only companies are permitted to use the words "limited," "limited liability," "incorporated," "corporation," "non-personal liability," or the abbreviations of these words. Those who contravene this section are liable to a fine of $50 per day for each day that business is done under the improper name (section 131).

You should note especially section 130(4) which renders officers and directors *personally* liable to indemnify persons who suffer a loss or damage as a result of being misled by the officers' failure to insist the company name be displayed on a document.

SAMPLE #12
REGISTER OF DIRECTORS

DIRECTORS

Name of Company J & J Industries Ltd.

NAME	RESIDENT ADDRESS		Date Appointed or Elected	Date Ceased	OFFICE HELD			
					Office	Date Appointed	Date Ceased	
John Doe	111 A Street Anywhere	B.C.	June 1/9–		President	June 29/9–		
Jack Doe	222 B Street Anywhere	B.C.	June 1/9–		Sec./Treas.	June 29/9–		

67

SAMPLE #13
REGISTER OF SHAREHOLDERS

REGISTER OF
SHAREHOLDERS

Name of Company ___ J & J Industries Ltd. ___   Page No. ___ 1 ___

Date Became a Member	Date Ceased to be Member	Full Name and Address	Representative Capacity	Class & Kind of Share	Par Value	Acquired by Allotments Conversion Transfer (or)	If Transferred From Whom	Cert. No.	Consideration Paid to Company			
									Agreed Per Share	Paid Per Share		
										Cash	Other than Cash	
											Amount	Pmts.
June 1 199–		John Doe 111 A Street Anywhere, B.C. Z1P 0G0	50	Comm.	NPV	Allot.		1	$0.01	$0.01		
June 1 199–		Jack Doe 222 B Street Anywhere, B.C. Z1P 0G0	50	Comm.	NPV	Allot.		2	$0.01	$0.01		

68

REGISTER OF SHARE ALLOTMENTS

REGISTER OF ALLOTMENTS

Name of Company ___ J & J Industries Ltd. ___   Page No. __1__

| Date of Allotment | To Whom Allotted Name and Address | Shares Allotted | | | | Consideration | | | | Commission or Discount per Share Allowed or Agreed to be Allowed |
		Quantity	Class and Kind	Par Value	Certificate Issued No.	Cash or Other Consideration	Amount Paid on Each Share	No. of Shares Allotted for Cash	No. of Shares Allotted for Other Considerations Particulars of Contract	
June 1 9–	John Doe 111 A Street Anywhere B.C. Z1P 0G0	50	Comm.	NPV	1	$0.50	$0.01	50		
June 1 9–	Jack Doe 222 B Street Anywhere B.C. Z1P 0G0	50	Comm.	NPV	2	$0.50	$0.01	50		
Aug. 3 9–	John Doe	100	Comm.	NPV	3	$50.00	$0.50	100		
Aug. 3 9–	Jack Doe	100	Comm.	NPV	4	$50.00	$0.50	100		

REGISTER OF TRANSFERS

Name of Company ___J & J Industries Ltd.___   Page No. _1_

Date	Certificate Surrendered			Name of Transferor	Name of Transferee	Certificate Issued		
	Kind & Class	Cert. Number	Shares			Kind & Class	Cert. Number	Shares
Aug 3 9—	Comm.	4	100	John Doe	Jean Doe	Comm.	7	50
Aug 3 9—	Comm.	5	100	Jack Doe	Jean Doe	Comm.	7	50

70

J & J Industries Ltd.

(the "Company")

We, the undersigned, being all the subscribers to the Memorandum and the first directors of the Company, hereby consent in writing to the following resolutions:

CERTIFICATE OF INCORPORATION

The Company was incorporated on the __1st__ day of __June__ , 19_9-_

under incorporation number __123 456__ .

COMPANY SEAL

RESOLVED that the Company seal, an impression of which is shown in the margin of these resolutions, be adopted as the common seal of the Company.

ALLOTMENT OF SHARES

RESOLVED that the following shares be allotted and issued to the subscribers at the price of __$0.01__ each as fully paid and non-assessable:

Cert. No.	Subscriber's Name	No. and Class of Shares
1	John Doe	50 Common shares without par value
2	Jack Doe	50 Common shares without par value

and that their names and other particulars in respect of such shares, be entered in the registers of allotments and members.

NUMBER OF DIRECTORS

RESOLVED that the number of directors of the Company be determined at __two (2)__ .

APPOINTMENT OF DIRECTORS

RESOLVED that the following persons, having consented in writing, be appointed the first directors of the Company:

John Doe
Jack Doe

AUDITOR

RESOLVED that the appointment of an auditor be waived pursuant to Section 203 of the Company Act until the first annual general meeting of the Company.

or

RESOLVED that _____ of _____
be appointed to act as auditor for the Company at a remuneration to be fixed by the directors of the Company.

ELECTION OF OFFICERS

RESOLVED that the following persons be appointed to the offices set opposite their respective names:

President : John Doe

Secretary/Treasurer: Jack Doe

QUORUM OF DIRECTORS

RESOLVED that the quorum for meetings of directors be fixed at __2__ .

BANKERS

RESOLVED that the directors open and maintain a bank account in the name of the Company at __Anywhere__
Credit Union, Main Branch, 100 Granville Avenue, Vancouver, B.C.

and that the resolution as to signing officers be annexed to these resolutions.

SHAREHOLDERS' LOANS

RESOLVED that the Company borrow the sum of __one thousand dollars ($1 000)__
from each of the member/directors and that the said shareholders' loans be secured by __Demand Notes__ .

RESOLVED that the Company execute the said __Demand Notes__ in such manner as to give full effect to the transactions hereinbefore described.

ACCOUNTING RECORDS

RESOLVED that the accounting records of the Company be kept at the Company's head office or principal place of business or at such other place as the director may from time to time determine.

INSPECTION TIMES

RESOLVED that, pursuant to section 188(5) of the Company Act, the examination of the records of the Company by any person other than the directors of the Company shall be restricted to two consecutive hours daily during normal business hours, namely, from 10:00 am to 12:00 noon each day.

TRANSFER OF ASSETS

RESOLVED that the Company purchase equipment as follows:

1. 1988 Chevrolet, Serial #123456JD89 from member/director John Doe $14 800.00.
2. 1979 Pontiac, Serial #98765SD12 from member/director Jack Doe $1 800.00.
3. Miscellaneous equipment and supplies from the members/directors jointly $500.00.

and that the said purchases shall be secured by Demand Notes.

RESOLVED that the Company execute the said ___Demand Notes___ in such manner as required to give full effect to the transactions hereinbefore described.

YEAR END

RESOLVED that the financial year end of the Company be ___December 31st___ of each year.

The foregoing resolutions are hereby consented to in writing by the subscribers to the Memorandum and the first directors of the Company.

Dated as of the 29th day of June, 199-.

John Doe
John Doe

Jack Doe
Jack Doe

6

COMPLYING WITH GOVERNMENT REGULATIONS

There are certain government licences and regulations that will affect you and your business. This chapter contains a summary of the things you need to know to keep your business and yourself in good standing with the government.

a. KEEPING ACCOUNTS

Books and records by your company will be audited by federal and provincial agencies from time to time. Therefore, you might as well establish from the beginning an orderly records and accounts system which will be readily accessible.

To do this you will need the help of a good accountant. The best way to find someone is to ask your successful business friends, people you admire in a business sense, to supply you with names. Then talk to at least three of them before making a choice.

If you want to learn something about accounting before you talk to an accountant so you can ask some intelligent questions, please refer to *Basic Accounting for the Small Business*, another title in the Self-Counsel Series, for a simplified explanation of the accounting process.

You can expect to have your books examined by the following government departments: Workers' Compensation Board, Revenue Canada — Taxation (which will include payroll auditing of unemployment insurance premiums, Canada Pension Plan contributions, income tax deductions at source), and Revenue Canada — Customs and Excise.

The provincial department of finance administers and will audit your books for social services tax.

You must keep your books and records, including supporting documents — such as sales and purchase invoices, contracts, bank statements, and cancelled cheques — in an orderly manner at your place of business or designated records office.

Revenue Canada — Taxation requires that you keep all business records and supporting documents until you request and obtain written permission from the department to dispose of them. If you wish to destroy company books or records, you must apply in writing to the director of the district taxation office in your area. You must also provide detailed information identifying the material and the fiscal period covered by such books.

Note: Some records must be kept indefinitely. These include the minute book, share records, general and private ledger sheets, special contracts and agreements, and the general journal if it is essential to the understanding of the general ledger entries. Other books must be kept until a tax audit or payroll audit has been completed or at least four years after the taxation year covered and at that time permission to destroy the records may be given.

b. FEDERAL REQUIREMENTS AND REGULATIONS

1. Goods and services tax

The goods and services tax (GST) is a value-added tax imposed by the federal government. Under the GST, a business collects tax from its customers. The tax is calculated as the sale price of taxable goods or services multiplied by 7%.

A *business* is entitled to claim a credit for any GST paid on the purchase of goods or services used in its business. This credit (an "input tax credit") is available to each business in the production and distribution chain. The final *non-business consumer* of the good or service does not get a tax credit for the GST he or she pays. The final consumer therefore bears the burden of the tax.

The total amount of GST collected in a given period, less the input tax credits for that period, must be remitted to Revenue Canada. If, in any given period, the input tax credits exceed the tax collected, a business will be entitled to a refund equal to the difference.

In general, all goods and services sold in Canada will be subject to GST. However, certain specified goods and services (such as basic groceries and health care) will not be taxable.

All businesses with gross sales in the preceding year that exceed $30 000 are required to register with Revenue Canada, Excise, for purposes of collecting and remitting GST on their sales.

A business with gross sales below $30 000 is known as a small supplier and registration is optional. Unregistered businesses are not required to charge GST on their sales but are unable to recover GST paid on their purchases. Therefore, even if your sales are under $30 000, you might want to register your corporation.

In order to claim the input tax credit, your corporation must keep detailed records of all GST it has paid out. There is an escape from this if you use the so-called "quick method" of GST accounting. (Use of the "quick method" is limited based on sales.) Under this method, you still collect the full 7% GST on your sales but you do not remit all of this to the government — instead you only send a portion to the government. You

cannot then claim the input tax credit or expenses, though you can still claim the credit on capital items.

For more information on how the GST will affect businesses, see the *The GST Handbook,* another title in the Self-Counsel Series.

2. Federal excise tax

An excise tax is imposed on certain specific goods, whether manufactured or produced in Canada or imported into Canada. The list of excisable items includes jewellery, matches, cigarettes, and tobacco. Complete details can be found in the Excise Tax Act, a copy of which may be purchased from the government's authorized bookstore agents.

Revenue Canada — Customs and Excise requires that all persons or firms manufacturing or producing goods subject to an excise tax operate under a manufacturer's excise tax licence. You can obtain this licence from the regional or district Excise Tax Office, Revenue Canada, in the area in which you or your company propose to operate.

Manufacturers licensed for excise tax purposes may purchase or import free from excise tax goods that are to be incorporated into and form a constituent or component part of an article or product that is subject to an excise tax, provided they quote their excise tax licence number and relevant certificate.

The procedure for filing returns and paying excise tax is similar to that for sales tax. If you are in any doubt concerning your status under the Excise Tax Act, write to the regional director of Revenue Canada — Excise Branch nearest you.

3. Customs duties

Any business that imports products from abroad must be aware of customs duties that are levied against goods upon entry into Canada. There are regulations concerning invoicing, classification of goods, rates of duty and reductions, and exemptions for special classes of articles.

If you are planning to import goods into Canada, you should obtain a ruling on the classification, rate of duty, and valuation prior to commencing shipments. If you are a foreign exporter or Canadian importer, you can either contact the regional collector of customs, Revenue Canada, which has jurisdiction over the Canadian port of entry for the majority of your goods, or a customs broker whom, if you intend to ship either in or out of the country, you will need anyway.

4. Federal income tax

The federal government levies both personal and corporate income tax on monies earned in Canada. Income taxes are applied on income received or receivable during the taxation year from all sources inside and outside Canada, less certain deductions. Individuals and branches of foreign companies carrying on business in Canada are also liable for income taxes on profits derived from these business operations. Small businesses qualify for special tax rates (see chapter 2 on tax tips for further information).

If you are an employer, you are required to deduct personal income tax from the pay cheques of all employees on a regular basis and remit these funds monthly through any branch of a chartered bank or to the Taxation Data Centre nearest you. You must start to deduct employee benefits when the employee begins to work for you.

The federal income tax regulations outline the rules for allocating income to provinces when individuals earn business income in more than one province.

For specific information about federal income tax, contact the nearest office of Revenue Canada — Taxation.

5. Unemployment insurance

In Canada, workers who become unemployed may qualify for unemployment insurance benefits under a federal government program. The program is administered by Human Resources Development Canada (formerly Employment and Immigration Canada).

With few exceptions, all employment in Canada performed under a contract of service is insurable, and, therefore, subject to unemployment insurance premium payments by both the employer and the employee.

The employer is required to collect employees' premiums in accordance with the current premium scales. All matters relating to deductions, remittances, and ruling for unemployment insurance premiums are handled by Revenue Canada — Taxation.

6. Canada Pension Plan

The Canada Pension Plan is designed to provide a basic retirement pension for working Canadians. Employees between the ages of 18 and 70 in most types of employment are covered by the plan and must contribute.

Types of non-pensionable employment include agriculture, horticulture, fishing, hunting, forestry, logging, or lumbering, where the employee earns less than $2 500 in cash per year.

The employer is responsible for making the deductions from salaries of eligible employees and must match these deductions with similar contributions. A person who is self-employed is responsible for the entire annual contribution to the Canada Pension Plan.

Note: If you are incorporated and pay yourself a wage, as far as the Canada Pension Plan is concerned, you are not self-employed. You should deduct the normal amount from your wage and the company will also contribute as the employer.

Revenue Canada — Taxation can help employers calculate the amount of unemployment insurance, Canada Pension Plan, and income tax deductions to be made from employees' salaries. When you apply for an account number, they will supply you with the charts to calculate the deductions, along with an explanatory book. The employer *must* remit these funds through any branch of a chartered bank or the Taxation Data Centre, Ottawa, Ontario.

c. PROVINCIAL GOVERNMENT REQUIREMENTS AND REGULATIONS

1. Licensing

There are certain specific provincial acts containing licensing regulations and requirements that apply to specific businesses. While it is impossible to list all the provincial acts and the businesses to which they apply, the following is a list of areas that fall under the provincial jurisdiction and about which you should be concerned if you operate a business in these areas.

(a) Door-to-door sales, pyramid schemes, franchises

(b) Firms that loan money or are involved in any way with the consumer finance business

(c) Manufacturers (especially regarding labor laws and factory standards)

(d) Anyone who handles or processes food

(e) Anyone who is in the transport (goods or persons) business

(f) Anyone who is dealing with the natural resources, such as forests, minerals, or water

(g) Anyone in the fish processing business

(h) Anyone who is affected by pollution standards

(i) Anyone who does business on provincially owned land, such as parks and beaches

2. The Workers' Compensation Board (WCB)

All incorporated businesses are required to register with Workers' Compensation. If you're in a partnership, coverage for you and your partner may be optional, but for your employees (including spouse and children), it is mandatory. So, if your spouse is your partner, you may be able to escape coverage.

Note: If you have a limited company, you are not self-employed as far as the Workers' Compensation Board is concerned. Your company is the employer; you are an employee. This means your spouse and children would also be covered as employees.

The amount you will pay depends on two things: the accident-prone "rating" of the industry you're in and the total payroll of your company. Even if you, as the principal shareholder, draw little or no salary, you may be "assessed" a higher salary level for purposes of Workers' Compensation Board coverage. This assessment must be paid totally by the employer. You cannot deduct a portion from the employee's wages.

When you register, you will be given your registration number, your payroll assessment rate, accident prevention regulations, and information on claims-reporting procedure.

Your assessments are used by the Workers' Compensation Board to provide rehabilitation services and financial and medical assistance to workers who are injured on the job. The act is meant to provide a way for the worker to receive assistance without having to go to court first to sue his or her employer or fellow employees. In most cases, people are entitled to benefits under the act, regardless of who was at fault in causing the injury.

What happens if you fail to register with the board? For one thing you are guilty of committing an offence and, if an employee is injured and his or her claim is allowed, your company will have to bear the cost of the claim in the form of an additional assessment. All unpaid assessments will have to be made up as well. If you are the principal of an unregistered company, you won't receive compensation for your injuries and you may be liable for a penalty.

Unpaid assessments constitute an unregistered lien on all real estate and on machinery or other goods owned by the company. They actually rank in priority over registered mortgages and other charges (like a mechanic's lien). The delinquent assessment fees may be recovered from your company when the asset is sold, or from any subsequent purchaser.

If you hire people classified as independent operators who work on a consulting or "freelance" basis, these people will not be considered your employees, and you may not be responsible for making the payroll assessments to the board for their wages. The kind of worker who can be classified as an independent operator varies depending on the business or industry. You should check with the board about anyone who does any work for you. Sometimes, even a casual laborer hired for just a few hours may have to be covered.

In any event, a pamphlet and application form will be mailed to the registered office of the company shortly after incorporation.

Be sure to contact your nearest WCB office for assistance and any additional information.

3. Sales tax

Every provincial government, with the exception of the one in Alberta, imposes a sales or social services tax. At present in British Columbia the tax is 7%, which is levied on virtually all tangible personal property that is purchased or imported for consumption or use. This tax is collected from the ultimate consumer by the seller.

If you are going to be buying merchandise for resale, you will need to apply for a provincial tax number. Upon application,

a registration certificate assigning a tax number will be issued by the provincial consumer taxation branch.

This certificate grants exemption from the payment of the tax on merchandise that is purchased for resale purposes or for merchandise that will become part of tangible personal property intended for resale.

d. MUNICIPAL GOVERNMENT REQUIREMENTS AND REGULATIONS

1. Licensing

The Municipal Act authorizes every municipality to license businesses within its boundaries. Incorporated centres issue licences and permits based on local bylaws. Communities can control aspects of zoning, land use, construction, and renovation for all types of business activities including the licensing of commercial vehicles.

Contact the local city hall or municipal office for information in these areas. In unincorporated areas, contact the nearest government agent or R.C.M.P. detachment.

2. Municipal taxes

Municipal governments levy direct taxes on real estate, water consumption, and business premises.

Property taxes are based on the assessed real value of the land and improvements. Annual notices of assessment are sent out with provision for appeal.

Local business taxes are applied directly against the tenant or the business operator. The business tax is generally a flat rate based on the number of employees you have.

However, some cities (notably Vancouver) assess on a percentage of the annual rental value, which can be a substantial amount.

3. Building requirements

All three levels of government have some responsibility for regulating commercial building. Any construction which is proposed must satisfy all the requirements of the three governments.

The city hall or municipal office brings together all the various building codes and inspections, making it possible for approval of planned construction to be obtained at the local level.

The municipality controls the type of building you may construct. Municipal building and zoning regulations control the physical structure and the final use of your building. The municipality also has the power to enforce building regulations.

Before beginning construction or renovation of a structure, you must obtain a building permit from the municipality. To apply, you must submit preliminary sketches for approval and, when the sketches have received approval, submit complete construction drawings which will be examined to ensure that they meet the federal, provincial, and municipal building standards. If approval is given, then you will be issued a building permit.

Once construction has been started, various stages of the construction must be inspected before the project can continue.

As each municipality controls certain aspects of construction, the requirements vary from one area to another, so you should contact the building department of your municipal government office for specific requirements.

e. MISCELLANEOUS MATTERS

1. The metric system

The Canadian government has established a policy of promoting the use of metric measurements throughout the country. Compliance is mandatory in some areas of business. For further information on how you should be using the metric system in your business, contact your provincial Department of Economic Development or write to:

> Measurement Information Division
> Consumer and Corporate Affairs
> P.O. Box 4000
> Ottawa, Ontario
> K1A 5G8

2. Weights and measures

The Ministry of Consumer and Corporate Affairs is responsible for the approval and initial inspection of all weighing and measuring devices, such as scales and fuel dispensers, that are used in trade.

The Weights and Measures Branch must inspect all new trade devices prior to first use. If you acquire used weighing equipment for commercial use, you should notify the Weights and Measures Branch. Those devices requiring installation before being inspected (e.g., vehicle scales), must be inspected on site when operational. Movable devices may be factory inspected prior to shipping and the department must be notified when this equipment is in place. It is necessary to report any relocation of the equipment to the department to ensure that regular inspections can continue to take place.

The period between inspections varies but is usually every two years. You are responsible for the cost of the initial inspections.

For further information or to arrange for an inspection, contact the nearest Weights and Measures office of the federal department of Consumer and Corporate Affairs.

3. Packaging and labelling

Any prepackaged consumer product, including food and inedible items, is subject to the packaging regulations of the federal Ministry of Consumer and Corporate Affairs.

Prepackaged products require a label stating the product's net quantity. The information must be declared in metric units and, optionally, in Imperial units of measure, and must appear in French and English. The identity of the product must also be given in both French and English.

In some instances, other information may be required. For example, hazardous or dangerous products must be properly marked, according to the Hazardous Products Act. Textiles must be labelled with the fibre content according to the Textile Labelling Act. This act provides for the mandatory labelling of such textile articles as wearing apparel, fabrics sold by the piece, and household textiles. It also regulates the advertising, sale, and importation of all consumer textile fabric products.

Articles such as jewellery, silverware, optical products, watches, pens, and pencils, which are made wholly or partly of precious metals, are regulated by the Precious Metals Marketing Act.

There are restrictions on the permissible size of the packages and for certain products only specific sizes are allowed. The federal Department of Consumer and Corporate Affairs should be contacted for detailed information regarding packaging.

4. Patents, copyrights, trade marks, and industrial designs

The laws concerning patents, copyrights, trade marks, and industrial designs are very complicated and you will find professional help useful.

Registered patent and trade mark lawyers specialize in these fields and consultation with them will ensure you get maximum assistance.

Inquiries about copyright, patents, trade marks, and industrial designs should be directed to:

Bureau of Corporate Affairs
Department of Consumer and Corporate
  Affairs, Canada
Place du Portage, Phase 1
Ottawa/Hull, Quebec
K1A 0C9
Tel: (819) 997-1936 (patents and
                trade marks)
    997-1726 (copyright and
               industrial design)

(a) Patents

A patent is a contract between the federal government and an inventor to exclude others from using the invention in Canada. Patents are granted for inventions that are defined as some technological development or improvement which has not previously been considered. The term of the patent is 17 years.

If you wish to apply for a patent, you must make an application to the Commissioner of Patents, Ottawa, Ontario. The application must meet all the requirements of the Patents Act and the Patent Rules. For more information, see *Patent Your Own Invention in Canada*, another title in the Self-Counsel Series.

If you have not yet completed your invention and are concerned that others might patent it, you may file a description of the invention as far as it has been developed with the patent office. The document filed is known as a caveat.

The caveat may also have some value in proving when your invention was made. It does not give you any right to exclude others from using the invention. It is not until you have filed an application for patent and been granted a patent that you are entitled to any exclusive rights to the invention. A caveat is not an application for patent, and its value is limited.

(b) Copyrights

The Canadian Copyright Act recognizes the exclusive right of an author to reproduce every original literary, musical, dramatic, and artistic work he or she creates, provided the author was a Canadian national, a British subject, or a citizen of a country that adhered to the Universal Copyright Convention when he or she produced the work.

The author's rights are recognized as existing once he or she has produced the work. This exclusive right lasts for the life of the author and 50 years after the author's death. In the case of records, discs, and photographs, the term of protection is 50 years irrespective of the life span of the author.

You are not required to register a copyright; you automatically own the copyright in your own works. If you wish to register a copyright, you must send your application to the Registrar of Copyrights in Ottawa on the form prescribed in the Copyright Rules. You must state your name, give the title of the work, and submit a registration fee payable to the Receiver General for Canada.

(c) Trade marks

The Trade Marks Act governs trade mark registration in Canada and provides for the registration of trade marks used in association with services or wares.

Registration, although advisable, is not compulsory; however, a registered mark is more easily protected than an unregistered trade mark.

A trade mark lasts for 20 years and is renewable. The Trade Marks Act outlines the types of symbols that can and cannot be used.

The application may be submitted by you, the owner of the trade mark, or your authorized agent. There are no forms for a trade mark application, but you must supply specific information and there is a fee of $150 for filing and a further fee of $200 after the application has been accepted. For more information on registering a trademark, see *Trade Marks: Questions and Answers*, a publication available from your library or for no cost from the government's authorized bookstore agents.

If you use a lawyer or registered agent (see *patent agent* in the Yellow Pages), it will cost anywhere from $400 to $2 000 to register a trade name and mark.

(d) Industrial designs

An industrial design is any original shape, pattern, or ornamentation applied to an article of manufacture. The article must be made by an industrial process.

An industrial design may be registered in Canada if the design is not identical or similar to others registered. The design must be registered within one year of publication in this country. Registration provides you with exclusive right to the design for a period of five years and it may be extended for one additional five-year period.

To register a design, you must file a drawing and description with the Registrar of Industrial Design in Ottawa. A search will be made of earlier designs to determine if the design is novel.

5. Product standards

Any product you make for sale in Canada will have to meet certain standards to ensure that it is safe and to protect the consumer against faulty construction and misleading sales practices.

Your product will probably have to be inspected by one of the following:

(a) The Canadian General Standards Board sets standards for products as diverse as hair-dryers and mobile homes. Most electrical goods must conform to its standards. For information, contact the CSA Testing Laboratories nearest you; you will find the office listed in the white pages of the telephone book.

(b) The Underwriters Laboratories of Canada sets standards for fire protection equipment, building materials, and related products. Their address is:

Underwriters Laboratories
  of Canada
7 Crouse Street
Toronto, Ontario
M1R 3A9
Tel: (416) 757-3611

(c) The Ministry of Consumer and Corporate Affairs, Legal Metrology Branch, is responsible for testing and approval of weighing and measuring devices that are used in trade.

(d) The Ministry of National Health and Welfare is responsible for all phases of selling, manufacturing, and importing foods, drugs, cosmetics, and medical equipment. Emphasis is placed on the control of plant facilities, ingredients, formulas, and packaging. For further information, contact the health protection branch in Ottawa or the district office nearest you.

For general information, you can also contact —

Standards Council of Canada
350 Sparks Street
Ottawa Ontario
K1R 7S8

6. Immigration and citizenship

If you are established in business in a foreign country but wish to live and establish a business in Canada, you must contact the Canadian immigration representative in your country.

You must apply for permanent resident status while you are still outside Canada. If you satisfy the immigration officer about the feasibility of your business proposal and you meet all other immigration requirements, it is possible that you will receive permanent resident status.

Canadian citizenship is usually not needed for employment in Canada except in certain areas of the civil service and some professions. If you are considering employment that is not just temporary, you must apply for permanent resident status before your arrival in Canada. Full citizenship can be applied for after three years' residence in Canada.

Canadian customs regulations allow the duty-free entry of personal property that is owned by people prior to coming to Canada. You may not sell or dispose of these goods within 12 months of your entry without paying duty.

If you plan to bring with you tools or machinery necessary for your business or profession, be sure to make arrangements before you have them shipped. Customs duty and sales tax are applicable to equipment, and you should be aware of the requirements.

Further information on the above may be obtained from the nearest Canadian embassy or consulate or by writing to Employment and Immigration — Canada in Ottawa. (See also *Immigrating to Canada*, another title in the Self-Counsel Series.)

7. Consumer protection

Unfair business practices are strictly regulated by both the federal and provincial governments, and you should be aware of your rights and obligations under the various laws.

In many provinces, for instance, high pressure selling may get you into trouble. You can write Consumer and Corporate Affairs and ask for their literature on the subject.

Check your provincial Consumer Affairs Bureau, if there is one, and contact the section of your provincial government that deals with business practices to get as much information as possible about the regulations that govern the way you are supposed to do business.

7
ALL ABOUT SHARES

a. KINDS OF SHARES

This is an area that causes problems for some do-it-yourselfers, but it is easy to understand once you realize that there are only two kinds of shares: par value and without par value. Both kinds of shares may be issued in different classes. For example, you can have preferred without par value shares, and cumulative par value shares.

There is really no practical difference between the two kinds of shares. Someone just puts an arbitrary value for the shares in relation to the worth of the company.

In most cases, you should incorporate with without par value shares so that you are not restricted to issuing your shares to subscribers or original shareholders for a set price, as you would have to do with par value shares.

You may issue the minimum of one share to each subscriber for 1¢ if you wish, and, if there are only two of you, it would mean that your company would start off with 2¢ in its share capital account.

The price at which you issue without par value shares to yourselves is strictly dependent upon the amount of equity capital you wish to establish. (See section **i.** below for a discussion of why you should not invest a large sum in the equity capital of a corporation.) The effect of the equation "net worth = value of shares" is not in any way affected by starting off with par value shares. This equation is always true, and if you wish to invest $1 in a company, it makes no real difference if you purchase one par value share for $1 or one hundred without par value shares for 1¢. The value of both types of shares will rise and fall in relation to the net worth of the company.

b. CLASSES OF SHARES

As most small non-reporting companies have no need for many different classes of shares, you may ignore this section unless you are curious.

A *share* represents a proportionate interest in the *net* value of a company (i.e., what would remain if all the company's liabilities to outside creditors were fully paid.) The person who owns the share, or shareholder, has a number of contractual rights as set out in the articles and memorandum of the company, as well as those rights set out in the Company Act.

Generally speaking, shares can have innumerable rights and restrictions attached to them. A class of shares is a set of shares that has attached to it rights different from the rights attached to another set of shares.

For example, when you start your business, you, like most people, should incorporate with an issue of "common shares" to all of the incorporators so that all the shareholders of the company have equal rights to vote and receive dividends.

When your company becomes successful, you might wish to create a different class of shares which, when issued to shareholders, will give them the right to receive dividends before holders of any other class of shares, or which have cumulative dividend rights, or rights to be redeemed by the company. You might refer to the new class of shares as "preferred" shares to distinguish them from the first group of shares. Large reporting companies usually have many different classes of shares.

Remember, it is much easier to add rights and restrictions at a later date rather than attach them now and have to buy them up or strip them later. If, at a later date, you wish to create classes of shares that have different rights attached to them, you should see a lawyer so you can carry out the alterations of your articles correctly and design your capital structure properly to minimize taxes and maximize control.

c. ISSUING AND CANCELLING SHARES

The issuing and cancelling of shares is a relatively simple affair because the form of share certificate is already prepared for you. You should be careful, however, to distinguish between the *initial issue* of shares on incorporation, *subsequent issues* out of the treasury (i.e., from the unissued "pool"), and *transfers* of already-issued shares from one person to another. All three of these dealings involve different operations. The transfer of shares is discussed in section **h.** below.

For the average small, non-reporting company, relatively few share certificates will suffice for normal purposes. This is because there are usually only a few shareholders and each share certificate can represent the total number of shares held by each person. (You do not need a separate certificate for each share.)

Share certificates should, whenever possible, remain in the minute book, because, if they are sent to the individual shareholder, some will inevitably be lost and you will then be faced with the annoying problem of replacing lost share certificates and the preparation of a statutory declaration detailing the loss. Share certificates no longer have to be issued under the seal of the company but they must be signed by at least one director or officer. Any other signatures may be printed or mechanically reproduced. Share certificates should be numbered consecutively in the space provided at the top of the certificate. The remaining information needed can be ascertained by closely examining the share certificate in Sample #17.

To cancel shares, simply write the word "cancelled" across the face of the certificate and staple it shut on top of the tab or stub of the certificate. (See Sample #18.)

Finally, you must prepare the appropriate directors' consent resolutions confirming the issuance or cancellation of shares. Actually, there should never be a cancellation unless there is, at the same time, a transfer, so the two would be incorporated into the same resolutions.

Examples of consent resolutions showing the initial issue of shares are shown in chapter 5.

d. INITIAL ISSUE OR ALLOTMENT OF SHARES

The initial issue of shares can be most simply handled by having all the intended shareholders sign the memorandum and place beside their names the number and kind of shares to be subscribed for.

The only problem with this method is that the first subscribers are automatically the first directors. If any of your initial shareholders do not wish to be directors, you will have to file a Notice of Directors with your other incorporation documents.

As all directors have considerable responsibility placed upon them, it would be wise for you to read the section "Duties and Liabilities of Directors," in chapter 11, before you subscribe to shares on the memorandum.

e. HOW MANY SHARES SHOULD YOU ISSUE?

In British Columbia, the capital structure of a company is not restricted by incorporation fees. This means that you can have any number of without par value shares or shares at

COMPANY .... J & J Industries Ltd. ....

SHARE CERTIFICATE

TRANSFER DETAILS

Cert. # ..... 1 ...... Class .Common.. No. of Shares.... 50 .....Par Value. No

Registered Name .... John Doe ....

Date entered in

Register of Members .... June 1 .... 19..9—

From: ....

To: ....

Received Certificate Number ....

this .... day of .... 19....

J & J Industries Ltd.

INCORPORATED IN THE PROVINCE OF BRITISH COLUMBIA

CERT. #	CLASS	NUMBER of SHARES	PAR VALUE	DATE NAME ENTERED IN REGISTER
1	Common	50	No	John Doe

.... is the registered holder

THIS CERTIFIES THAT .... John Doe ....

of ...Anywhere...British.Columbia..

of ...Fifty..(50).Common..................... Shares,

in the Authorized Capital of

transferable only in the Register of Members, and in accordance with the Articles of the Company, by completion of the Form of Transfer endorsed hereon and surrender of this Certificate.

IN WITNESS WHEREOF the Company has caused this certificate to be signed by

its duly authorized officer(s) this ...... 29th .... day of ..... June ...... 19...9...

John Doe

.... President ..... John Doe .....

TITLE

TRANSFER OF THESE SHARES IS RESTRICTED.

SAMPLE #18
CANCELLED SHARE CERTIFICATE

COMPANY .... J & J Industries Ltd.

SHARE CERTIFICATE

Cert. # ....1..... Class ..Common.. No. of Shares... 50 ...Par Value... No...
Registered Name ......John..Doe..
Date entered in 19.9-
Register of Members ...June.. 1 - ....

TRANSFER DETAILS

From:..................................
To:......................................
Received Certificate Number ....
this................................ day of .... 19.....

CERT. #	CLASS	NUMBER of SHARES	PAR VALUE	DATE NAME ENTERED IN REGISTER
1	Common	50	No	June 1, 199-

THIS CERTIFIES THAT ....John..Doe..
of ....Anywhere,. British. Columbia. .... is the registered holder
of ....(50). Common. .... Shares,
in the Authorized Capital of ....J & J Industries Ltd.

(INCORPORATED IN THE PROVINCE OF BRITISH COLUMBIA)

transferable only in the Register of Members, and in accordance with the Articles of the Company,
by completion of the Form of Transfer endorsed hereon and surrender of this Certificate.
IN WITNESS WHEREOF the Company has caused this certificate to be signed by
its duly authorized officer(s) this ....29th......... day of ..... June 19--

John Doe
President...John..Doe.......
TITLE

TRANSFER OF THESE SHARES IS RESTRICTED.

CANCELLED

86

a par value that can range anywhere from 1¢ to $100 per share.

However, there is no need in most simple incorporation situations to immediately issue all of the shares. The unissued shares remain in the company treasury and belong to it until it becomes necessary to issue them to new shareholders.

Although you may feel that issuing and selling many shares is a good idea because it will bring money into your corporation and make it worth more, this is not correct. The number of shares issued does not affect the real value of your company. The simplified examples in Samples #19 and #20 illustrate this.

In Sample #19, the company issued 100 shares at $1 each. The company has earned $4 000 to date. Therefore, its total net worth is $100 (original investment) + $4 000 (earnings) for a total of $4 100. However, as $100 of this amount is shareholder's money and it is really a matter of transferring it from one hand to the other, it should not be included in determining the value of the corporation for the shareholders. So deduct the original $100 investment from the net worth. If the corporation were liquidated tomorrow, it would actually be worth $4 000 in net returns to the shareholders.

In Sample #20, the company issued 10 000 shares at $1 each. The company has earned $4 000 to date. Therefore, its total net worth is $10 000 (original investment) + $4 000 (earnings) for a total of $14 000. But, again, as described above, we deduct the original investment of $10 000 from the net worth, leaving the same $4 000 in net returns to the shareholders if the company was liquidated tomorrow. On a net return basis, the company is worth the same whether it issues 100 or 10 000 shares.

When deciding how many shares you should issue, there are several important points to remember.

First, when issuing shares initially, it is the proportion of shares each shareholder receives that is important, not the number. For example, if you are the only shareholder, you could issue yourself one share at $10 000 each or 10 000 shares at $1 each. Either way, your company ends up with $10 000 and you own 100% of the shares.

If there are two shareholders and they are to own the company equally, the company can issue each shareholder ten shares or 5 000 shares; the number is unimportant as long as the equal proportion is maintained.

Second, it may be more convenient in some cases to issue a larger number of shares rather than a smaller (i.e., several thousand rather than a few dozen). This way, it will be easier to sell any of these shares to another person, because each share will have a lower value. Similarly, it will be easier for a newcomer to your company to subscribe for shares from the company treasury since each share will have a lower value than if only a few were issued. For example, if you and your partner each invest $1 000 in your company, you could issue to each of you ten shares at $100 each or 10 000 shares at 10¢ each. If you chose to issue shares at $100 each, however, a share purchaser with only $50 could not buy any shares.

Finally, keep in mind that there is good reason not to issue all the shares of your company and to retain some in your treasury. This strategy allows flexibility as your company grows and changes. Consider the situation where a new shareholder will be joining the corporation.

If you had issued all the shares in the company, you would have to transfer a percentage of each existing shareholder's shares to the new shareholder. In order to do this, you could easily end up with "fractional shares." For example, John and Jack Doe are the only shareholders in their company and each holds 50 shares. They decide to bring in Helen as an equal shareholder. To do this, both Jack and John have to sell

SAMPLE #19
BALANCE SHEET
(Where 100 shares are issued)

J & J INDUSTRIES LIMITED

Assets		Liabilities	
Cash	$ 100	Note to the bank	$2 000
Inventory	4 000	Shareholder loan	3 000
Building	5 000		
Total assets	$9 100	Total liability	$5 000
		Net worth	
		Capital stock authorized — 10 000 shares	
		Issued 100 shares at $1 each	100
		John Doe — 50 shares	
		Jack Doe — 50 shares	
		Retained earnings	4 000
		Total equity	4 100
		Total liability and equity	$9 100

Note: The corporation has earned $4 000 to date. Each share is worth $41 (total net worth divided by 100) but as $100 of this amount is shareholders' money, and it is really a matter of transferring it from one hand to the other, it really should not be included in determining the value of the corporation from the shareholders' point of view. Therefore, if the corporation were liquidated tomorrow, it would be worth $4 000 in net returns to the shareholders.

SAMPLE #20
BALANCE SHEET
(Where 10 000 shares are issued)

J & J INDUSTRIES LIMITED

Assets		Liabilities	
Cash	$10 000	Note to the bank	$2 000
Inventory	4 000	Shareholder loan	3 000
Building	5 000	Total liability	$5 000
Total assets	$19 000		
		Net worth	
		Capital stock authorized — 10 000 shares	
		Issued 10 000 shares at $1 each	10 000
		John Doe — 5 000 shares	
		Jack Doe — 5 000 shares	
		Retained earnings	4 000
		Total equity	14 000
		Total liability and equity	$19 000

Note: If the business is wound up, John and Jack Doe's shares are worth $14 000, but $10 000 of this is their own money. Therefore, the net return would again be $4 000.

88

16⅔ shares to Helen and each party is left with 33⅓ shares, an awkward situation.

If, however, there were still unissued shares remaining in the treasury, you could either issue extra shares to the existing shareholders that they could in turn sell to the new shareholder, or simply issue new shares directly to the new shareholder.

So, in the example above, the company would issue 25 more shares each to John and Jack, who could then sell those to Helen, leaving all three shareholders with equal shareholdings of 50 shares each. John and Jack could choose to sell the new shares to Helen at a higher price, but if they did so, they might trigger capital gains tax. If they chose to sell the shares to Helen for the same price as they paid, the tax department might consider that a taxable benefit to Helen and tax her.

If the shares were issued directly from the treasury to Helen, no tax would be triggered, and, of course, John and Jack would make no actual profit from bringing Helen in, because the money paid by Helen goes into the corporation and not to John or Jack.

Another major reason for not issuing all of the shares is that even if they were issued at 1¢ each, if 10 000 shares were available, it would cost the shareholders another $100 that has to be put into the company's bank account at the time of incorporation. There is no advantage in financing the company by this method.

f. SUBSEQUENT ISSUE OR ALLOTMENT OF SHARES

Questions often arise over what price the shares should be valued at when a new partner is buying into the company. In a reporting company, where the shares are publicly traded, there is no problem establishing the price. In a non-reporting company, it is more difficult. The Company Act allows the directors to issue new shares at whatever price they wish (subject to section 42 — see below). However, there may be tax implications for the new partners receiving shares of a business if the shares are issued at less than market value.

Most small businesses would rather not hire some outside business consultant to "value" the shares. And if, as is often the case, the new partner is brought in because of the expertise he or she can contribute to the business, he or she often does not pay full market value for the shares.

The Income Tax Act states that if a new shareholder pays less than fair market value for shares, then the balance is called a "taxable benefit" and must be included in the new shareholder's income for the year in which the shares are received as a capital gain.

Obviously, there are problems for the tax department questioning this type of valuation in a small, non-reporting company. However, should they audit your company's return and reassess the person involved, it is up to the taxpayer to disprove the tax department's position, which is difficult to do. There are some legal steps around this problem, such as claiming as reserve against the "gain" or having the new shareholder purchase an "option" at a much lower price instead of the shares themselves, but all of these steps require some assistance from a professional and really go beyond the scope of this book. If this situation applies to you, you will need some expert advice.

Note: An employee may buy new shares at any price without being considered to have received a taxable benefit. The only requirement is that the employee keep the shares in his or her name for two years. When the shares are sold, the difference between the actual purchase price and the sale price is a capital gain. This tax advantage offers employees the opportunity to buy a substantial interest in their company for very little money and receive a valuable employee benefit.

The act gives existing shareholders *pre-emptive rights* on new issues of shares. This simply means that the existing shareholders have the right to maintain their *proportionate* positions in relation to the other shareholders on a new issue of shares.

For example, J & J Industries Ltd. initially allotted 50 shares to John Doe and 50 shares to Jack Doe. If the directors decided to issue a further 200 shares (the directors being, in this case, the same persons) each shareholder would have the right to take up to a further 100 shares.

The practical effect of all this is that each shareholder can maintain his or her position in relation to the other shareholders.

In many cases, because the shareholders and directors are the same persons, all parties agree to a new issue of shares and the pre-emptive rights are a welcome reform measure because, too often in the past, the right to make new issues of shares was effectively used to water down the rights of minority shareholders.

Section 41 of the Company Act outlines the procedure for issuing shares out of treasury. It states that the directors of a non-reporting company must, before allotting the shares, offer them pro rata to the existing shareholders.

After receiving a subscription as shown in Sample #21 for an allotment of a specific number of shares, existing shareholders must sign a consent and waiver as shown in Sample #22 before resolutions in writing can be drawn up to allot the shares, as shown in Sample #23.

Before issuing new shares you should also be aware of section 42 which states that par value shares may not be issued for less than their par value. In the case of shares without par value, the directors may determine their price as authorized by part 3.7 of the Articles. Section 47 provides that a discount may be allowed or commission paid on issues of without par value shares.

If you plan to issue more shares and if the present shareholders will not sign waivers, you must comply with the procedures laid down in section 41 of the act. The highlights of the procedure are as follows.

Section 41(3) directs that an offer must be made in writing to each shareholder which specifies the number of shares and time for acceptance. The time for acceptance must not be less than seven days but may be longer at the discretion of the directors.

Section 41(4) allows the directors to sell the shares to whomever they wish if the time lapses with no notice of acceptance or they receive a notice of acceptance or they receive a notice declining the offer from one or more shareholders. However, the directors cannot sell to third parties on terms that are more favorable than those offered originally.

Directors may not issue fractional shares, or shares that have not been fully paid for in cash or *past* services. A promissory note is not sufficient.

g. ISSUING SHARES IN TRUST

Probably the most common reason for issuing shares in someone else's name and having him or her sign a trust agreement is that some provincial legislation requires a shareholder to be either a resident or a citizen of the province. In this case, shareholders are forced to use "front" people to hold the shares. In British Columbia, there is no such requirement. However, a majority of directors must be Canadian citizens or permanent residents and at least one director must be a British Columbia resident.

h. TRANSFER OF SHARES

This refers to the simple transfer of issued shares from one shareholder to one or more other shareholders.

Transfers are regulated by the company's articles and our model set deals with transfers in detail in Article 24. Basically, as in a new issue of shares, Article 24

SAMPLE #21
SUBSCRIPTION

TO: J & J INDUSTRIES LTD.
AND TO: The Directors thereof

    The undersigned hereby subscribe for and agree to take Common shares without par value in the capital of the above captioned company set opposite our respective names at the price of $0.50 per share and enclose herewith the sums of $50.00 each payable to the company in full payment of the aggregate price of said shares.

DATED this 12th day of September, 199-.

Name	Number of Shares
John Doe	100 Common shares without par value
Jack Doe	100 Common shares without par value

_____John Doe_____   _____Jack Doe_____
JOHN DOE   JACK DOE

SAMPLE #22
CONSENT AND WAIVER FOR ALLOTMENT OF SHARES

J & J INDUSTRIES LTD.
(the "Company")

CONSENT AND WAIVER

In consideration of $100.00, we the undersigned, being all the holders of all the issued common shares in the authorized capital of the Company, hereby consent to the allotment of the following common shares without par value to the following persons at the price of $0.50 each and do waive any and all rights that we may have pursuant to the Memorandum or the Articles of the Company or the "Company Act," (R.S.B.C. 1979 Chapter 59 and amending acts) with respect to such allotment:

Name	No. and Class of Shares
John Doe	100 Common shares without par value
Jack Doe	100 Common shares without par value

DATED this 12th day of September, 199-.

_____John Doe_____   _____Jack Doe_____
JOHN DOE   JACK DOE

provides that the remaining shareholders have the right of first refusal to purchase the seller's shares and also that the remaining shareholders have the right to purchase them on a pro rata basis as regards the other shareholders. If the remaining shareholders decline to purchase the offered shares, they should sign a Waiver and Consent as shown in Sample #24.

At this point, the offeror may —

(a) decline to sell the shares not accepted,

(b) offer the remaining shares (if any) to the shareholders who accepted the first offer, again on a pro rata basis, or

(c) sell the remaining shares (if any) to third parties, but he or she may not sell them on more favorable terms than contained in the offer to the other shareholders.

Article 24 outlines the procedure in further detail. The shareholder who is selling shares completes the transfer form on the back of the share certificate (see Sample #25). A directors' resolution transferring the shares is then prepared (see Sample #26) along with the new share certificate. Check the new share certificates to make sure the number of shares they represent equal the number of shares represented by the cancelled share certificates.

For example, John Doe owns 150 common shares of J & J Industries Ltd. represented by share certificate number 1 for 50 common shares and share certificate number 3 for 100 common shares. Jack Doe owns 150 common shares of J & J Industries Ltd. represented by share certificate number 2 for 50 common shares and share certificate number 4 for 100 common shares. John Doe transfers the 50 shares represented by share certificate number 3 to Jean Doe and Jack Doe transfers the 50 shares represented by share certificate number 4 to Jean Doe. If the new shareholder is also going to be appointed a director, a Consent to Act as a Director (see Sample #27) and a Member's Consent Resolution (see Sample #28) are prepared. A Notice of Directors is sent to the Registrar of Companies (see chapter 12).

In many cases, an issue and transfer of shares will take place at the same time, especially when a new "partner" is being brought into the company and the existing shareholders wish to realize a capital gain on the sale of part of their business. In this case, the procedures regarding consents and notices have to be complied with, but the resolutions of directors that confirm the issue and transfer can be combined into one.

Your company is empowered to redeem shares that have a right of redemption attached to them and to purchase its own shares in accordance with the provisions of sections 259 and 260. However, the company must not repurchase or redeem shares when it is insolvent or if such action would cause the company to become insolvent.

Furthermore, a non-reporting company must offer to purchase its shares from shareholders on a pro rata basis the same way it must issue shares on a pro rata basis.

If your company is considering the purchase of some of its shares to reduce its capital base, professional advice should be sought because of the tax ramifications of such a purchase.

Finally, the discussion in section e. on tax considerations regarding issue or allotment of shares also applies to transfers. If in doubt about tax ramifications, always consult a tax expert.

i. SHOULD YOU SELL SHARES OR BORROW FUNDS TO FINANCE YOUR COMPANY?

After a new corporation is organized, it may require financing to begin operations. One way you can raise money for your corporation is by issuing and selling shares to yourself or someone else.

DIRECTORS' RESOLUTION APPROVING ALLOTMENT OF SHARES

J & J INDUSTRIES LTD.
(the "Company")

We, the undersigned, being all the directors of the Company, hereby consent in writing to the following resolutions:

WHEREAS subscriptions have been received from the persons listed below for the allotment to them of the number of shares of the class and at the price set opposite their names:

Name	No. and Class of Shares	Price per Share
John Doe	100 Common shares	$0.50
Jack Doe	100 Common shares	$0.50

RESOLVED:

(1) that the Company having received full payment do allot, issue, and deliver to the persons listed above, the number of shares and at the price per share as set opposite their respective names and such shares be declared to be fully paid and non-assessable:

(2) that the following share certificates be issued:

Share certificate #	Name	No. and Class of Shares
3	John Doe	100 Common shares
4	Jack Doe	100 Common shares

and that any director or officer of the Company execute the said share certificates and deliver them to the persons entitled thereto.

DATED this 14th day of September, 199-.

_____
JOHN DOE

_____
JACK DOE

93

TO: J & J INDUSTRIES LTD.
AND TO: The directors thereof

The undersigned, being all the registered holders of shares in the capital of the company, hereby irrevocably waive any and all right to be offered any of the shares which the directors propose to transfer as follows:

Transferor	Transferee	Number and class of share
John Doe	Jean Doe	50 Common shares
Jack Doe	Jean Doe	50 Common shares

Dated the 3rd day of August, 199-.

_____
JOHN DOE

_____
JACK DOE

CERTIFICATE

FOR

One hundred (100) Common   SHARES

REGISTERED IN THE NAME OF

John Doe

CAPITAL

J & J Industries Ltd.

I,   John Doe

of   111 A Street, Vancouver, B.C.

in consideration of the sum of $1.00

Dollars paid to me by Jean Doe

of   333 C Street, Vancouver, B.C.

(hereinafter called the "Transferee"), do hereby transfer to the Trans-

feree   Shares in the undertaking called

fifty (50) Common

    J & J Industries Ltd.

to hold unto the Transferee, Jean Doe, and her
executors, administrators and assigns, subject to the several conditions on
which I held the same at the time of the execution hereof, and the
Transferee in taking delivery hereof takes the said shares subject to the
conditions aforesaid.

As Witness my hand the   3rd   day of   August
A.D. 19 9—

TRANSFEROR _____ *John Doe*

WITNESS _____ *Walter Witness*

J & J INDUSTRIES LTD.

The undersigned, being all the directors of the company, hereby consent to and adopt in writing the following resolutions:

TRANSFER OF SHARES

RESOLVED that a proper instrument of transfer having been received, the following transfer of shares be approved:

Transferor	Transferee	Number and class of share
John Doe	Jean Doe	50 Common shares without par value
Jack Doe	Jean Doe	50 Common shares without par value

CANCELLATION OF SHARE CERTIFICATES

RESOLVED that pursuant to the foregoing transfer of shares, the following share certificates be cancelled:

Share certificate #	Name	Number and class of shares
3	John Doe	100 Common shares without par value
4	Jack Doe	100 Common shares without par value

ISSUE OF NEW SHARE CERTIFICATES

RESOLVED that pursuant to the foregoing transfer of shares, the following share certificates be issued:

Share certificate #	Name	Number and class of shares
5	John Doe	50 Common shares without par value
6	Jack Doe	50 Common shares without par value
7	Jean Doe	100 Common shares without par value

RESOLVED that a director of the company is hereby authorized to execute and deliver the above share certificates.

RESOLVED that the appropriate entries be made in the company's Register of Members and Register of Transfers.

DATED the 3rd day of August, 199-.

_____
JOHN DOE

_____
JACK DOE

SAMPLE #27
CONSENT TO ACT AS A DIRECTOR

I, John Doe, of 111 A Street, Anywhere, B.C.; hereby consent to act as director of J & J INDUSTRIES LTD. this consent is effective until revoked.

John Doe
_____
JOHN DOE

DATED as of the 1st day of June, 199-.

SAMPLE #28
CONSENT RESOLUTIONS OF MEMBERS APPOINTING A NEW DIRECTOR

J & J INDUSTRIES LTD.
(the "Company")

We, the undersigned, being all the members of the Company, hereby consent in writing to the following resolutions:

1.   RESOLVED that the number of directors of the Company be changed from two (2) to three (3).

2.   RESOLVED that Jean Doe be appointed as a director of the Company effective the 15th day of June, 199-, such person having consented in writing to act as a director of the Company.

DATED as of the 3rd day of June, 199-___

John Doe   _Jack Doe_
_____   _____
JOHN DOE   JACK DOE

If you will be the investor, however, there are definite disadvantages to capitalizing a business through the purchase of shares rather than through a loan, especially in a high-risk business starting in a newly incorporated corporation.

Money invested in shares cannot be easily recovered while the corporation is operating; therefore, any recovery of money by the owners must be achieved through wages or dividends, which are taxable in the recipient's hands. Capital *loaned* to the corporation, as opposed to *invested* in the corporation, can be recovered at any time, tax free (i.e., a loan to the corporation repaid to a shareholder is not taxable income to the shareholder). (The interest earned on the loan, however, is taxable.)

In addition, should the corporation collapse, repayment to the shareholders for money invested in shares ranks behind any kind of loan, including a shareholder loan. While a shareholder loan ranks equally with the other creditors when dividing up the remainder of the assets, common share holders rarely see any proceeds when a company goes bankrupt. Therefore, you are more likely to recover your money if you have loaned it to the company rather than using it to purchase shares.

If, on the other hand, the investors will be other businesspeople, it might be advantageous to your company to sell them shares rather than borrow money from them. In this way —

(a) the company has no corporate obligation to repay the money unless and until the company is dissolved, and

(b) the company's balance sheet will appear stronger with more money in the "equity" column and less in the "debt" column.

If you or another shareholder wish to loan money to your company, simply write the company a cheque and make a note on the cheque and bank deposit slip that it is a shareholder loan. The cheque stub will then show the information for your accountant or bookkeeper to make the proper entries in your ledgers.

It is always a good idea to draw up a promissory note or demand note recording the amount of the loan and the interest, if any, payable on it. Your promissory note should state whether the amount of money is to be payable whenever the lender calls for it (a demand note), or is to be paid off over a period of time in instalments.

An example of a demand note is shown in chapter 8 on transferring assets. Banks and legal stationers carry many preprinted ones as well. Be sure to read them over carefully before using them. They are very simple to draw up. Be certain that a fixed sum is payable on a certain date or at a certain time. The making of the promissory note by the corporation should be approved of in either resolutions of directors or in minutes of a directors' meeting. The note and the approving resolutions or minutes would then be filed in the company's minute book.

8
TRANSFERRING ASSETS TO A NEW COMPANY

a. THOSE WRITE-OFFS

Many people who incorporate believe that a company that owns assets is in a more favored position with regard to tax write-offs (i.e., depreciation and expenses) than an individual. This is not true.

Take, for example, the company car. If the company owns the car and you use it for business purposes, the company is entitled to deduct operating and depreciation expenses as a valid business expense. If you also use the company car for pleasure, this value is calculated and added to your taxable income as a benefit received (i.e., it is not a free benefit to you).

At present, the Income Tax Act states you must include in your personal income an amount equal to 2% per month of the purchase price of the vehicle if you use a company car for pleasure, or two-thirds of the lease cost if it is leased by your company. If, however, your personal use of the vehicle is less than 1 000 kilometres per month, the standby charge is reduced.

The theory is that you are entitled to use a company vehicle on company business, and the company is entitled to deduct expenses while the vehicle is used in this manner. Your use of the car for other than company business is a taxable benefit to you, and the company may not deduct expenses while the vehicle is used for the pleasure of one of its employees. Just because some employees succeed in using their company cars equally for business and pleasure and avoid declaring the personal benefits they receive does not mean that this proposition is invalid.

On the other hand, if you own the vehicle and use it in the course of employment with a company, you would be entitled to deduct the business portion of operating expenses and depreciation from your personal income. In other words, you would be classified as an independent "contractor" who "rents" a car to the company. Usually you would receive a separate allowance for the use of your car while on the job. You would be surprised at how many employees, like travelling sales representatives, operate on this basis and actually profit from the use of their cars.

The important thing to remember is that both the company and the individual are entitled to deduct legitimate expenses incurred in the use of such assets, and where you have an "incorporated partnership" in which employees and shareholders are the same persons, it makes no difference whether the company or the individual receives the benefit of these write-offs.

Actually, there may be a slight difference, depending on the individual situation, because of the variance in individual and corporate tax rates. However, this is usually not significant enough to justify a wholesale transfer of assets into the company.

There are, however, other benefits to be granted from transferring assets into the company at the time of incorporation. First, the transfer psychologically "locks" the partners into the company in that each makes a commitment to the new venture by "selling" an equal amount of assets to the company. Also, it makes the accounting easier. It is simplest for the company to own the asset and deduct depreciation and operating expenses. If an employee owns the asset and rents it to the company, both the employee and the company will have to keep records of expenses.

b. PROVINCIAL TAX PROBLEMS

You may transfer assets into a newly incorporated corporation without having to pay provincial sales tax if, at the time of the transfer, the transferor or the transferor and spouse own 95% of the issued shares.

The same situation applies in the case of a partnership provided the partners retain the same proportionate interest in the newly incorporated company as they had in the assets of the partnership. For example, if a truck were owned by a partnership of three (excluding spouse) and they wished to transfer it to a company in which only two people were shareholders, the company would have to pay sales tax on one-third of the value of the truck. If all three individuals held an equal number of shares, then no sales tax would be payable.

The time period allowed for tax-free transfers is flexible but you can usually count on a grace period of a month or two from the date of incorporation. If you think that the actual transfer will be delayed for some reason, it might be a good idea to record the transfer of the asset in the minutes of the first meeting of directors. This provides evidence of your intent.

If you attempt to transfer personally owned assets to the company much later than two months after incorporation, the company will have to pay sales tax on the value of the item.

c. FEDERAL TAX PROBLEMS

If you are rolling over an existing business into a company or incorporating yourself and selling assets to the company, you have to be careful to avoid certain federal tax complications. This is because under the law you and the company that you control are not dealing at arm's length. In other words, you are not strangers to each other and the potential for setting up artificial transactions is something the tax department watches out for. When a sale is made in a non-arm's length transaction, the Income Tax Act requires the selling price to be at fair market value.

In situations where you have been depreciating assets for tax purposes, this can lead to your being personally liable for tax through the recapture of capital cost allowance. In other words, say you have been operating a proprietorship that owns a delivery van valued on the books at $2 000. Perhaps in reality, this van is worth $3 000. You must value the van at that price when you sell it to your company. This would create a recapture situation of $1 000, which would have to be included in your income in the year that the transfer was made and on which you would pay taxes.

To avoid this kind of situation, there is a special section of the Income Tax Act (section 85) which provides for a "roll over" election. The effect of this election is that it allows you to place artificial figures on the selling price of assets to avoid a change in your tax situation. In other words, in the example above, you would elect to transfer the delivery van to your company at a value of $2 000 instead of the fair market value of $3 000.

There is a similar provision for the sale of real estate, and to take advantage of this, you should consult your accountant. The forms involved are easy to follow, but the decisions regarding the value of the assets you are selling to the company are sometimes complicated. So, if you are in the situation where you are transferring property consisting of real estate that you had owned previously, or assets which have been depreciated for tax purposes, see your accountant first.

d. METHODS OF TRANSFER

In any transfer of an asset, two things must be kept in mind:

(a) It must be transferred at a fair market value.

(b) There must be adequate proof of the transfer for the federal (income) and provincial (social services) tax departments.

The whole transaction is subject to review by the income tax department and transfers of assets at inflated values are usually caught sooner or later. Sometimes the tax people may want an independent appraisal and if you are able to produce proof of the appraised value, it will greatly strengthen your case.

As far as any car, truck, or other self-propelled industrial equipment that falls under the Motor Vehicles Act is concerned, you will require documentation in the consent resolutions plus the usual motor vehicle transfer forms.

To obtain the tax exemption for motor vehicles, you must visit your local Consumer Taxation Branch of the British Columbia Government, and take along your consent resolutions evidencing the transfer. They will issue you an exemption form and you may then go to the Motor Vehicle Branch and complete the transfer forms.

Other assets may be transferred by simply recording the fact in the resolutions of a meeting of directors. If there are a great many items and/or a large amount of money involved, you should draw up a Bill of Sale (forms are available at most stationery stores) and file a copy in the company minute book.

e. FINANCING THE TRANSACTIONS

When you sell your asset to your company, the company must give something back in return as a payment for the debt. It is better to receive a debt obligation than shares in exchange for your asset because, when the company pays off its debts, you can receive the money tax free as the repayment of your loan. If you receive shares, your assets are forever tied up in the company and you will receive no direct benefits unless the company is wound up and the assets are sold at a profit, which is highly unlikely. The most common form of payment is the demand note, as shown in Sample #29.

A note like this should be prepared on behalf of the company in favor of each person transferring assets into the company.

As you can see, John Doe is entitled to "demand" payment at any time. Well, what is to stop Mr. Doe from demanding payment immediately? First, he is not likely to demand payment unless he knows there are sufficient funds in the company's bank account to pay him. Second, if he had to sue, it would be tantamount to suing himself since he is the part owner of the "entity." So, you see, a demand note payable to a member-director of an incorporated partnership is a relatively safe proposition. Usually an informal agreement between the working "partners" about where and when the notes should be presented for payment is quite sufficient.

If the company pays interest on the note to Mr. Doe, he has to pay tax on it. Interest payments made to the holder of the note are taxable in the noteholder's hands. The principal amount is not taxable as it is analogous to the repayment of a loan made to the company.

There is one major taxable risk in transferring assets to a company. If the company goes bankrupt or has judgments registered against it, the assets may be subject to seizure by the trustee in bankruptcy or the judgment creditor. If this happens, the debt owed to you by the company would be relegated to general creditor status and you would have to share in the proceeds of the resale of the assets along with the other creditors.

This happens infrequently, though, because you can usually foresee these events, in which case you may make demand on your note and seize the asset(s) in the event of the company's non-payment. In doing this you should be aware of a little-known law called the Fraudulent Preferences Act which says no one may transfer or convey property with the intention of defeating creditors. There is a three-month time limit from the date of the transfer within which the creditor must apply to upset the transfer of the property from your company to you.

If you intend to transfer many valuable assets, it would be wise to transfer the goods subject to a chattel mortgage or conditional sales agreement. You are then elevated to the level of secured creditor if there are other claims made on the assets. The mortgage or conditional sales agreement must be registered in the Companies Office, the particulars of the mortgage inserted in your register of debentures, and a copy of the mortgage filed in your minute book. A lawyer will draw up either agreement for you.

SAMPLE #29
DEMAND NOTE

$2 000   September 30, 199-

ON DEMAND after the above date the company promises to pay to the order of JOHN DOE at Vancouver, British Columbia, TWO THOUSAND DOLLARS ($2 000) with interest at the rate of fifteen percent (15%) per annum, as well after as before maturity, FOR VALUE RECEIVED.

J & J INDUSTRIES LIMITED

Per: "JOHN DOE"
President

"JACK DOE"
Secretary

9

DO YOU NEED A BUY-SELL AGREEMENT?

A buy-sell agreement is simply an agreement among the shareholders of a company that, on the happening of a certain event (usually the death or resignation of one of the "partners"), one or more of the remaining shareholders will purchase the shares of the deceased or departing person.

The purpose of the agreement is to enable the existing shareholders to retain control of the company. The death of a shareholder in a "close corporation" or "incorporated partnership" type of company creates a serious situation for both the estate of the deceased shareholder and the surviving shareholders of the company.

From the point of view of the estate of the deceased shareholder, the shares of the company held by the deceased shareholder may have no market as outsiders will seldom buy such shares unless the business is an established one and they are able to purchase the majority interest in the company. The only persons who may be interested in buying the shares may be the surviving shareholders. But, if the deceased had a minority interest in the company, the surviving shareholders would retain control anyway. Thus they would have no real interest in buying the shares and, therefore, have the power to force the estate to sell the shares at bargain prices.

From the point of view of the company, it may be very important to prevent the sale of the shares by the estate to a stranger or to someone with whom the remaining shareholders do not get along, or to prevent the shares from being held by the beneficiaries of the deceased shareholder. The death of a shareholder in a close corporation with no prior agreement on the disposition of the shares may also adversely affect the credit position of the company because of the uncertainty as to the future of the business.

The only effective solution to these problems is for all the shareholders of the company to enter into a "buy-sell agreement." Under this type of agreement, the estate of a deceased shareholder is obligated to sell and the surviving shareholders are obligated to purchase all of the shares of the deceased at a specified price or at a price to be determined under the agreement. Buy-sell agreements have the advantage of relative simplicity except where there are more than two or three parties, when this type of agreement can become very complicated.

Buy-sell agreements present two major problems:

(a) The funding of the purchase of the shares

(b) The valuation of the shares of the deceased

Usually, the purchase of the shares is funded by business life insurance policies under which each shareholder insures the lives of his or her fellow shareholders, naming himself or herself as beneficiary of each policy.

The idea is that the surviving shareholders will use the insurance proceeds to purchase the shares of the deceased shareholder from the estate of the deceased shareholder.

There are, of course, different types of life insurance and the decision as to which

103

type should be obtained by the parties, the amount of insurance, and other related matters should be made only after consultation with an experienced life insurance underwriter.

The other problem may be dealt with in a number of ways as no single method of valuation is appropriate to all types of business operations or circumstances. There are four general methods by which shares can be valued —

(a) by some form of fixed formula (book value, capitalization of earnings, etc., or a combination of two or more of these methods),

(b) by some form of appraisal or arbitration,

(c) by a fixed dollar amount by agreement among the parties, with or without a provision for periodic revaluation, or

(d) by a combination of two or more of these methods.

In an incorporated husband and wife business, you can divide the shares according to each party's contribution. Ideally, however, a buy-sell agreement should be drawn up which provides that one person should buy up the other according to a predetermined formula. Determining this formula is often the greatest difficulty in making one of these agreements. You may wish to use a coin toss to decide which party is to buy out the other if there are two people who are equally capable of running the business. The proceeds of a cashed-in life insurance policy may be used to finance the purchase.

Whatever the terms of the agreement, it is a good idea to have this matter settled before a marriage breaks up. Many people have made the unfortunate discovery that it is extremely difficult to make maintenance payments to someone out of earnings derived from a company that is disrupted by disagreements between its directors. Too often, if no agreement is reached, the company is wound up and both parties experience unnecessary economic loss.

By adopting a buy-sell agreement, the parties are bound to resolve this messy situation according to a predetermined formula — one that can be enforced in the courts if need be.

The form of buy-sell agreement shown in Sample #30 is a very simple one and is provided only as a sample of what might be included in one. I strongly suggest you obtain competent legal advice if you wish to enter into a buy-sell agreement.

BUY-SELL AGREEMENT made the _____ day of _____ , 19 _____ ,

between _____ of the _____[city]_____ of _____ ,

in the _____[province]_____ of _____ (herein called

_____) and _____ , of the said _____[city]_____

of _____ (herein called _____).

WHEREAS:

(1) The parties own or control all the issued and outstanding shares in _____ Corporation Limited (herein called "the Corporation") as follows:

[Set out shareholdings]

(2) The parties desire to provide for their mutual protection if either dies or wishes to withdraw from the Corporation.

THIS AGREEMENT WITNESSES that the parties covenant and agree as follows:

1. The parties shall not transfer, encumber or in any way deal with any of their shares in the Corporation except as provided for in this agreement.

During the lifetime of the parties

2. If either _____ or _____ wishes to dispose of his shares in the Corporation, he (herein called the "Offeror") shall first offer in writing to sell all his shares to the other party (herein called the "Offeree") on the following terms and conditions:

3. The offer shall contain:

(a) an offer to sell all the shares of the Corporation owned or controlled by the Offeror (herein called "all his shares" or "the shares") at the price and on the terms stipulated in the offer;

(b) an offer to purchase all the shares of the Corporation owned or controlled by the Offeree (herein called "all his shares" or "the shares") at the same price and on the same terms;

(c) an undertaking to close the purchase or sale on a date fixed not less than [eighty (80)] days and not more than [one hundred (100)] days from the service of the offer on the Offeree at the time and place fixed in the offer;

4. If the Offeree accepts the offer to sell under paragraph 3 the Offeror (herein called "the Vendor") shall sell and transfer all his/her shares to the Offeree (herein called "the Purchaser") who shall purchase and pay for them on the date and at the place stated in the offer for the price stipulated in the offer.

5. If the Offeree accepts the offer to purchase under paragraph 2(b), the Offeree (herein called "the Vendor") shall sell all his/her shares to the Offeror (herein called "the Purchaser") who shall purchase and pay for them on the date and at the price stated in the offer for the price stipulated in the offer.

6. If the Offeree does not accept either of the alternative offers in accordance with the provisions, he shall be deemed to have accepted the Offeror's offer to sell all his shares to the Offeree and the Offeree (herein called "the Purchaser") shall puchase and pay for them on the date and at the price stated in the offer for the price stipulated in the offer.

7. At the time set for closing, the Vendor shall deliver to the Purchaser in exchange for the items set out in paragraph 8:

(a) certificates for all his shares duly endorsed in blank for transfer;

(b) his resignation from the board and that of his wife and nominees, if applicable;

(c) his resignation as an employee and that of his wife and members of his family who may be in the employ of the Corporation;

(d) an assignment to the Purchaser of all debts, if any, owing the Corporation to the Vendor;

(e) a release of all claims the Vendor has or may have against the Corporation and the Purchaser;

(f) assignment of all insurance policies on the life of the purchaser as set out in Appendix A;

(g) a certified cheque payable to the Purchaser for an amount equal to the aggregate of the cash surrender value of all policies on the life of the Vendor as set out in Appendix A;

(h) all other documents necessary or desirable in order to carry out the true intent of this agreement.

8. At the time set for closing, the Purchaser shall deliver to the Vendor in exchange for the items set out in paragraph 7 above:

(a) a certified cheque payable to the Vendor for the full amount of the purchase price of the shares;

(b) a certified cheque payable to the Vendor for the full amount of any indebtedness owing by the Corporation to the Vendor as recorded on the books of the Corporation and verified by the Corporation's accountant;

(c) a certified cheque payable to the Vendor for an amount equal to the aggregate of the cash surrender value of all policies on the life of the Purchaser as set out in Appendix A;

(d) a release by the Corporation of all debts, if any, owing by the Vendor to the Corporation;

(e) a release of all claims the Corporation and the Purchaser have or may have against the Vendor;

(f) a release of all guarantees given by the Vendor on behalf of the Corporation;

(g) all securities, free and clear of all claims, which belong to the Vendor and are lodged with any person (including the Corporation's banks) to secure any indebtedness or credit of the Corporation;

(h) assignments of all insurance policies on the life of the Vendor as set out in Appendix A;

(i) all other documents necessary or desirable in order to carry out the true intent of this agreement.

9. If on the closing date the Vendor neglects or refuses to complete the transaction or does not comply with the procedures herein set out, the Purchaser has the right upon such default (without prejudice to any other rights that he may have), upon payment by him of the purchase price (plus or minus any adjustments herein provided) to the credit of the Vendor in any chartered bank in the [city] of _____ (or to the solicitor for the Corporation in trust for, on behalf of and in the name of the Vendor), to complete the transaction as above. The Vendor hereby irrevocably constitutes the Purchaser his true and lawful attorney to complete the said transaction and execute on behalf of the Vendor every document necessary or desirable in that behalf. [If there is more than one vendor, this power of attorney shall apply to both vendors.]

10. If on the closing date the Purchaser neglects or refuses to complete the transaction, or does not comply with the procedures herein set out, the Vendor has the right upon such default (without prejudice to any other rights that he may have) to give to the Purchaser, within ten (10) days after such default, notice that on the twenty-first day after the original closing date, he (herein called "the New Purchaser") will purchase from the Purchaser (herein called "the New Vendor") all the shares of the Corporation owned or controlled by the New Vendor, for an amount equal to seventy-five per cent (75%) of the purchase price set out in paragraph 8(a) and at the same time fix a new date within thirty (30) days and a time and place for closing; whereupon, on the new date for closing, the New Vendor shall sell all his shares to the New Purchaser who shall purchase the same for the new purchase price, and it is expressly agreed that all the terms of this agreement applicable to the closing of the sale and purchase of shares and to the adjustment of purchase price, if any, shall be applicable to the said closing. The New Vendor hereby constitutes the New Purchaser his true and lawful attorney to complete the said transaction and execute on behalf of the New Vendor every document necessary or desirable in that behalf. [If there is more than one vendor, this power of attorney shall apply to both vendors.]

11. No offer hereunder shall be given while another offer is outstanding or a sale pending or until [one hundred (100)] days after any sale is aborted.

After the death of a party

12. Within [one hundred (100)] days of the death of either _____ or _____ (provided the survivor is alive on the thirtieth day after the death of the first deceased) the survivor (Purchaser) shall purchase and the estate of the deceased (Vendor) shall sell to the survivor all his shares owned or controlled by the deceased at the time of his death for the most recent price stipulated in the offer.

13. The legal representatives of the deceased shall in writing fix a date not more than [one hundred (100)] days from the date of death a time and place for the closing of the sale of its shares.

14. At the time set for closing, the Purchaser shall deliver to the Vendor/Estate in exchange for the items set out in paragraph 15:

(a) a certified cheque payable to the Vendor/Estate for the full amount of the purchase price as set out in the offer.

(b) a certified cheque payable to the Vendor/Estate for the full amount of any indebtedness owing by the Corporation to the deceased;

(c) a certified cheque payable to the Vendor/Estate for the amount of the cash surrender value on all insurance policies on the life of the Purchaser listed in Appendix A;

(d) a certified cheque payable to the Vendor/Estate for the amount, if any, by which the aggregate net proceeds received by the Purchaser from the insurers in Appendix A exceeds the aggregate of (a), (b) and (c) above;

(e) a release by the Corporation and the Purchaser of all debts and other claims that they have or may have against the Vendor/Estate;

(f) a release of all guarantees given by the deceased Vendor on behalf of the Corporation;

(g) all securities, free and clear of all claims, belonging to the deceased Vendor which are lodged with any person (including the Corporation's banks) to secure any indebtedness or credit of the Corporation;

(h) all other documents necessary or desirable in order to carry out the true intent of this agreement.

15. At the time set for closing, the Vendor/Estate shall deliver to the Purchaser in exchange for the items set out in paragraph 14:

(a) certificates for all the Vendor's shares duly endorsed for transfer in blank with signature guaranteed by a bank or trust company;

(b) evidence of authority of executors to sign;

(c) succession duty release for the shares if applicable;

(d) resignations from the board and employment of all members of the deceased's family and nominees;

(e) an assignment to the Purchaser of all debts, if any, owing the Corporation to the Vendor;

(f) a release of all claims the deceased Vendor or his estate may or may have against the Corporation or the Purchaser;

(g) an assignment to the Purchaser of all insurance policies on the life of the Purchaser listed in Appendix A;

(h) all other documents necessary or desirable in order to carry out the true intent of this agreement.

Insurance

16. In order to ensure that all or a substantial part of the purchase price for the shares of the deceased party will be available immediately in cash upon his death, each of the parties hereto has procured insurance on the other's life as set out in Appendix A. Additional policies may be taken out for the purposes of this agreement and they shall be added to Appendix A.

17. Each of the parties hereto agrees, throughout the term of this agreement, to maintain and pay the premiums as they fall due on the life insurance policies listed in Appendix A owned by him.

18. The insurers set out in Appendix A are hereby authorized and directed to give any party hereto, upon written request, all information concerning the status of the said policies.

19. If any premium on any insurance policy is not paid within [twenty (20) days] after its due date, the party insured shall have the right to pay such premium and be reimbursed therefor by the owner thereof together with interest at the rate of [two] per cent per month on the amount so paid in respect of such premium from the overdue payment until the date of reimbursement.

20. Immediately upon the death of one of the parties hereto the survivor shall proceed as expeditiously as possible to collect the proceeds of the policies on the deceased party, and the legal representatives of the estate of the deceased party shall apply and expedite the application for letters of administration or letters probate, as may be required.

21. The parties shall not assign, encumber, borrow upon or otherwise deal with any of the insurance policies set out in Appendix A.

General

22. The parties shall not throughout the term of this agreement and until a valid sale of the shares is completed under this agreement do or cause or permit to be done anything out of the normal course of business of the Corporation.

23. Time shall be of the essence of this agreement and everything that relates thereto.

24. The parties agree to execute and deliver any documents necessary or desirable to carry out the true purpose and intent of this agreement.

25. This agreement shall be binding upon and enure to the benefit of the parties hereto and their respective heirs, executors, administrators and assigns.

IN WITNESS, *etc.*

SIGNED, SEALED AND DELIVERED, *etc.*

[Signatures and seals]

APPENDIX A

_____ CORPORATION LIMITED

BUY-SELL AGREEMENT

APPENDIX A

Life insurance policies on the life of _____ owned by _____:

Insurer   *Number*   *Amount*

Life insurance policies on the life of _____ owned by _____ :

Insurer   *Number*   *Amount*

ALTERNATE VALUATION CLAUSES

Valuation by auditor — Book value at fixed date

The survivor and the executors or administrators of the deceased shall cause a valuation of all other shares of common and preferred stock of the Corporation to be made by the auditors of the Corporation based on the book value of the Corporation on the first day of the month immediately preceding the deceased's death. If within thirty days the survivor and the executors or administrators of the deceased have not signified their approval of the valuation of the shares of the Corporation as determined by the auditors, the value of such shares shall be fixed by a board of three arbitrators selected as follows: the survivor shall select one arbitrator, the executors or administrators of the deceased shall select one arbitrator and the two so selected shall select the third arbitrator and the decision of a majority of the said arbitrators as to such valuation shall be final.

Book value — Capitalization of fixed assets

To the book value of the shares of the Corporation shall be added an amount equal to [six] times the difference between the average net profit of the Corporation, after payment of all taxes and dividends for [three] complete fiscal years of the Corporation immediately preceding the deceased's death and [ten] per cent of the adjusted net asset value of the Corporation as above determined at the date of the death of the deceased.

10
ANNUAL GENERAL MEETING AND ANNUAL REPORT

a. ANNUAL GENERAL MEETING

Although it is good business practice to hold regular annual meetings, the legal requirement amounts to a bothersome formality for most companies. Therefore, I recommend dispensing with the legal requirement by having all the shareholders sign the consent resolutions shown in Samples #31 and #32 and entering them in the minute book.

If you decide to appoint an auditor, you may appoint a certified management accountant, a certified general accountant, or a chartered accountant. Reporting companies, according to section 204, may rely only on the latter two types of accountants. Most non-reporting companies do not need the services of an auditor and generally waive the appointment.

You may want to consider taking on the extra expense of an audit in the following circumstances:

(a) When you or a co-owner are not involved in the day-to-day running of the company

(b) When the shareholders are not the same people as the managers

(c) When there are a large number of shareholders and an audit would reassure them of the company's position as well as protect the officers who are making accounting decisions

(d) When the volume of business transactions is so large that it is hard for one person to keep on top of it all

(e) When considerable borrowing is necessary (banks may require an audit)

If you are using the services of an auditor, professional advice should be sought on all proceedings.

b. ANNUAL REPORT

The annual report is a simple form which is required to be filed with the Registrar of Companies every year the company is in operation.

The office of the Registrar of Companies in Victoria will automatically forward a two-part annual report form to you (see Sample #33), which will include information up to the date of the previous annual report. You should make changes (if any) to bring the report up to date, sign it, and send it in. Don't forget to file a copy in your minute book.

Section 356 provides that the annual report must be filed within two months of each anniversary of the company's incorporation date and must contain the correct information as of the anniversary date. The filing fee for the annual report for either a reporting or a non-reporting company is $35.

Also, section 281 provides that if a company fails to file an annual report for two years, the Registrar shall institute steps to have the company struck off the record. This can be serious if the company owns valuable assets like land. If the company is not a company in good standing, it cannot sell any land it owns until it becomes reinstated. This is a time-consuming and very expensive procedure because all of the missing annual reports must be filed and a court application made to re-register the company. It is better to keep your filings up to date and avoid these problems.

SAMPLE #31
CONSENT RESOLUTION IN LIEU OF ANNUAL GENERAL MEETING

J & J INDUSTRIES LTD.
(the "Company")

We, the undersigned, being all the members of the company, hereby consent in writing to the following resolutions in lieu of an annual general meeting:
RESOLVED that:

1. Pursuant to Section 203 of the Company Act, the appointment of an auditor for the ensuing year be waived.
2. The presentation of financial statements of the Company for the last fiscal year be waived.

OR

1. The financial statements prepared and approved by the Company's auditor have been presented to each member.
2. All acts, contracts, proceedings, appointments and payments of money by the directors of the Company since the last annual meeting as appear in the proceedings and records of the Company be and the same are hereby approved, ratified and confirmed.
3. The following persons be elected as directors of the Company until the next annual meeting, having received a consent to act in writing from each:
    Jack Doe
    John Doe
    Jean Doe

DATED as of the 1st day of June, 199- by all the members who would have been entitled to attend and vote at the annual general meeting.

_____
JOHN DOE

_____
JACK DOE

SAMPLE #32
DIRECTORS' CONSENT RESOLUTION TO APPOINT OFFICERS

J & J INDUSTRIES LTD.
(the "Company")

Pursuant to the Company Act, the following resolutions are passed by the directors of the company, consented to in writing by all the directors of the company:

RESOLVED that the following persons be elected officers of the company until the next annual general meeting:

John Doe — President   Jean Doe — Vice-President
Jack Doe — Secretary/Treasurer

DATED as of the 1st day of June, 199-.

_____
JACK DOE

_____
JOHN DOE

_____
JEAN DOE

SAMPLE #33
ANNUAL REPORT FORM

Province of British Columbia	Ministry of Consumer and Corporate Affairs	ANNUAL REPORT	PAGE 1	PAGES 1
	REGISTRAR OF COMPANIES	FORM 18 (COMPANY ACT)		OF

SEE REVERSE BEFORE ENTERING ANY INFORMATION. PLEASE TYPE FORM.

CERTIFICATE NUMBER	DATE OF INCORPORATION, AMALGAMATION OR CONTINUATION	THIS REPORT CONTAINS INFORMATION AS AT	IS THIS A REPORTING COMPANY?
123 456	June 1, 199–	June 1, 199–	No

J & J Industries Ltd.
111 A Street
Anywhere, B.C.
Z1P 0G0

REGISTERED ADDRESS

FOR COMPANIES BRANCH USE ONLY

[X] NOT CHANGED

[ ] CHANGED, ATTACH A FORM 4 IN DUPLICATE AND A CERTIFIED COPY OF THE DIRECTORS' RESOLUTION

ANNUAL GENERAL MEETING WAS

[ ] HELD ON ____ 19__ AT __
DATE SHOULD BE DURING THE PRECEDING 13 MONTHS, OR IN THE CASE OF THE FIRST ANNUAL GENERAL MEETING DURING THE PRECEDING 15 MONTHS.

OR

[X] WAIVED, DEEMED TO HAVE BEEN HELD. June 2 19 9–
DATE SHOULD BE DURING THE PRECEDING 13 MONTHS, OR IN THE CASE OF THE FIRST ANNUAL GENERAL MEETING DURING THE PRECEDING 15 MONTHS.

SURNAME	GIVEN NAME & INITIALS	RESIDENTIAL ADDRESS (P.O. BOX, RURAL ROUTE, GENERAL DELIVERY NOT ACCEPTABLE)	POSTAL CODE
DIRECTORS			
Doe	John	111 A Street Anywhere, B.C.	Z1P 0G0
Doe	Jean	333 C Street Anywhere, B.C.	Z1P 0G0
Doe	Jack	222 B Street Anywhere, B.C.	Z1P 0G0
OFFICERS			
Doe President	John	111 A Street Anywhere, B.C.	Z1P 0G0
Doe Vice-president	Jean	333 C Street Anywhere, B.C.	Z1P 0G0
Doe Secretary/treasurer	Jack	222 B Street Anywhere, B.C.	Z1P 0G0

[X] NO [ ] YES ATTACH FORM 10 & 11

ANY CHANGES OF DIRECTORS

CRC004 R1082

CERTIFIED CORRECT

▷ *Jack Doe*
SIGNATURE OF OFFICER OR DIRECTOR

June 27, 199–
DATE

112

11
ALL ABOUT MEETINGS

a. GENERAL MEETINGS

If your articles provide for it, or if you are a one-person company, a quorum of one can constitute a meeting, according to section 165.

Your annual general meeting, if you have one, must be held within 15 months of incorporation, and thereafter no more than 13 months later than the date the last meeting was held, or waived, but at least once every calendar year.

Your meeting must be held within the province, and all members are entitled to receive at least 21 days' notice, or 56 days' notice if directors are to be elected.

If you waive the meeting, you must file the notices of waiver in your minute book, as well as a copy of your annual report.

Section 171 allows a shareholder holding not less than one-twentieth of the issued shares to require that a general meeting be held by giving a written "requisition" notice to the directors and by complying with certain other procedures.

There is no restriction on the reasons needed for calling such a meeting. Accordingly, in most small non-reporting companies, practically any shareholder will be able to legally enforce the calling of a meeting, although as a matter of practice forced meetings will likely be a rarity.

b. DIRECTORS' MEETINGS

Under the act, the directors hold virtually total authority for the operation of the company. Therefore, there will likely be numerous occasions when a directors' meeting is necessary.

Directors' meetings *must* be held in the following circumstances:

(a) When there has been an addition, deletion, or substitution of director(s) or shareholder(s).

(b) When a director has an interest in a proposed contract or transaction between the company and another party or company, in which case the director must disclose the nature and extent of his or her interest at the meeting (section 144). (This is the "conflict of interest" situation.)

(c) When a director holds any office or possesses property which might create a conflict of interest with his or her position as director, in which case full disclosure is also required (section 147).

(d) When the directors propose to sell, lease, or otherwise dispose of a substantial part of, or all of, the undertaking of the company (section 150). A special resolution of shareholders consenting to the transaction is also required.

(e) When the company is repurchasing some of its issued shares.

The above items are specifically discussed in the Company Act as requiring some sort of joint director action. In practice, it would probably be wise to call a directors' meeting whenever a matter of substantial business importance arises because of the liability and responsibility of directors.

There is one way in which the directors' business may be conducted without holding these meetings, and that is provided for in section 149, which states as follows:

149. Unless the articles require an actual meeting, any resolution of the directors, or of any committee of them, may only be passed without a meeting if all the directors, or the members of the committee, as the case may be, consent to the resolution in writing and the consent is filed with the minutes of proceedings of the directors or the committee.

As there are no provisions in our model set of articles *requiring* the directors to hold a meeting, this section would seem to permit the directors to dispense with meetings altogether provided the proper resolutions are filed and consented to (see part 15.12 of articles).

A meeting may be very informal. Some jurisdictions even allow a "meeting" over the telephone. The important thing here is to draw up the proper minutes, have them signed, and file a copy in the minute book.

c. MEMBERS' OR SHAREHOLDERS' MEETINGS

There are relatively few situations outlined in the act or articles where a shareholders' meeting is a must. However, you would be wise to call a shareholders' meeting whenever you feel directors are getting into "deep water" because of the extent of their personal liability for their actions as directors. A shareholders' mandate would almost certainly cure any act of the directors on behalf of the company as long as it was done honestly and in good faith.

Traditionally, shareholders' meetings were restricted to the annual general meeting where, in a private non-reporting company, their function was to approve the actions of the directors for the preceding year. Now, the annual general meeting can be waived by the shareholders, so there is no shareholders' meeting required as a part of the normal operation of the company.

However, there must be a meeting of members or consent resolutions in writing for an ordinary resolution or a special resolution to be passed (see ordinary and special resolutions defined in section 1 of the Company Act) when member approval is needed on specific procedures such as altering the memorandum by changing the company name, increasing, decreasing or changing the authorized share capital. Special resolutions are also required for selling or disposing of substantially all of the company's assets, amalgamating, continuing into another jurisdiction, altering the articles, etc.

Take a look at section 184 and you will see that the need for meetings per se is practically dispensed with in that no minutes need be taken in the case of passing an ordinary or special resolution when it is consented to in writing, in accordance with the procedure outlined in the definitions. Again, the consent resolutions must be filed in the company's minute book.

12
ALL ABOUT DIRECTORS AND OFFICERS

a. HOW MANY DIRECTORS AND OFFICERS DO YOU NEED?

Every non-reporting company needs at least one director. One of your directors must be ordinarily a resident of British Columbia and a majority of the directors must ordinarily reside in Canada.

You will need a president and a secretary as officers, who shall be different people, except, of course, in the case of a one-person company. The president must also be a director in all companies. Of course, your articles may make provision for a large number of officers.

b. WHAT CHARACTERISTICS MUST THEY HAVE?

The qualifications for directors are set out in detail in section 138 of the Company Act. Basically, a director must be 18 years old or older. He or she may not be an undischarged bankrupt, a corporation, or a person suffering from mental infirmity.

Furthermore, a person who was convicted of an offence involving fraud concerning the promotion, formation, and management of a corporation must wait five years from the sentence imposed in relation to the offence. This section applies to officers' qualifications as well.

c. HOW TO APPOINT DIRECTORS AND OFFICERS

In most non-reporting companies, the articles govern the appointment and discharge of directors. The act gives shareholders in a reporting company the right to propose nominees for directors and have pertinent information circulated with the management information circular that is sent around prior to an annual general meeting. At least 10% of the shareholders must support the proposal before the management is obligated to inform the other shareholders. British Columbia has no provision for cumulative voting in the election of directors like other provinces have.

The directors have complete authority to appoint and discharge any officers, *unless the articles provide otherwise*. (They never do.) Remember that the president must also be a director. If your company has two or more shareholders, it must also have at least two officers (a president and secretary).

Unless there is a change of directors or a subscriber to the memorandum does not wish to become a director, you need file no further forms with the Registrar on incorporation.

Remember that appointed directors must be present at the meeting at which they are elected or have consented previously to the appointment in writing. Sample #27 shown in chapter 7 is an example of such a consent.

When you appoint a new director, remember to file a Notice of New Directors (see Sample #34) with the Registrar within 14 days of his or her appointment. The filing fee for a Notice of New Directors is $20 and a true copy costs $25.

d. HOW DO YOU REMOVE A DIRECTOR OR OFFICER?

Other than at the annual general meeting, a special resolution (three-quarters vote) by all the shareholders is needed to remove

SAMPLE #34
NOTICE OF NEW DIRECTORS

PROVINCE OF BRITISH COLUMBIA

———

FORM 10 AND 11
(Sections 137 and 156)

———

Certificate of Incorporation No. <u>123 456</u>

COMPANY ACT

———

NOTICE OF NEW DIRECTORS

The following persons became directors of the undermentioned company on the date stated, namely:

Date <u>January 23, 199–</u>

Company <u>J & J Industries Ltd.</u>

Full names of new directors:
Jean Doe, 222 B. Street, Anywhere, B.C. Z1P 0G0

The following persons ceased to be directors of the above-mentioned company on the date stated, namely:

Date <u>January 23, 199–</u>

Full names of persons who have ceased to be directors:
Jack Doe, 222 B. Street, Anywhere, B.C. Z1P 0G0

The full names and resident addresses of all the directors of the company at the date set out below are:
John Doe 111 A Street, Anywhere, B.C. Z1P 0G0
Jean Doe 222 B. Street, Anywhere, B.C. Z1P 0G0

Dated the <u>28th</u> day of <u>January</u>, 19 <u>9–</u>

(Signature) _John Doe_

President
(Relationship to company)

116

a director from office. If the shareholders of a reporting company remove a director (see Article 14), it is important they remember the practical implications of the management contract that the company probably entered into with the director. The dismissed director may be able to enforce this contract or seek damages for dismissal because of the contract. This can make things pretty expensive.

Officers may be dismissed by a majority vote of the directors.

At the annual general meeting, all the directors are deemed to have resigned and a new slate elected. In most cases, the old directors are appointed to a new term by the consent resolution shown in Sample #31 in chapter 10.

e. THE POWERS OF MANAGEMENT

The Company Act contains a considerable number of provisions that directly touch on the structure, powers, and responsibilities of corporate management. These provisions mainly clarify the existing state of the law and practice in this area while others impose responsibilities upon directors and officers that increase their chances of incurring personal liability.

Directors are able to do almost anything on behalf of the company. If you look at part 12.1 of the articles you will see that it effectively restates the principle that the board has the most corporate powers. The board is so powerful that it is doubtful whether a majority of shareholders could overrule a decision. Furthermore, as the non-reporting company is empowered to purchase and redeem its own shares, you can see the opportunities directors have to manipulate share values and protect their positions. This problem should not be common in a non-reporting company because the directors and shareholders are nearly always the same people.

The directors are obligated to call a shareholders' meeting when proposing the disposal of the company's undertaking, but they may make major changes in the company and make charitable gifts at their own discretion without seeking shareholder approval.

The directors may not avoid having a meeting by using signed resolutions unless they unanimously consent to the resolution (section 149). If any director dissents, he or she will have to call a meeting so that the resolution may be passed by the majority of the directors and the dissent noted by the secretary in the minutes of the meeting. British Columbia directors are allowed the privilege of having telephone meetings.

f. DUTIES AND LIABILITIES OF DIRECTORS

So you are a director. Even though your board meetings are held at the kitchen table, your duties are the same as those of directors who sit around a long teak table surrounded by graphs and plush carpets.

You should read this discussion of directors' duties even if you are only an officer, like a secretary or treasurer, because the same responsibilities are imposed on you by virtue of section 159. Read sections 142 to 148 of the act so that you may fully understand these duties.

1. Consideration

Directors are prohibited from issuing shares until the company receives full consideration for those shares. The consideration may be money, *past* services, or property (land or machinery, etc.). The directors may determine the value of the consideration by resolving that in all the circumstances of the case, the property or service is provided to the company at the fair market value. It is no longer possible to issue shares in consideration for someone's promissory note or future services. See sections 43 and 44 of the act for full details.

A director is required to act honestly, in good faith, and in the best interests of *the company*. He or she is also required to exercise the care, diligence, and skill of a reasonably prudent person. All officers of the company have the same duties imposed on them.

2. Conflict of interest

The act deals with the problems of conflict of interest and duty by making directors and officers who contract with their companies or have an interest in a contract with the company disclose to the other directors the nature and extent of their interest at the first meeting in which the contract is discussed, or, on failing to disclose promptly to the board, the interested director or officer must disclose his or her interest to the shareholders.

The shareholders must approve the contract by special resolution, and the contract must be fair and reasonable when the company enters into it. This may seem to put a director or officer in a precarious position: the shareholders may approve the contract, but a court at a later date may decide that the contract was not fair and reasonable, so the director may be left wondering for a long time whether or not he or she is entitled to keep the profit from any contract in which he or she was interested.

The duty to disclose is an onerous one but it *must* be met if a director is to avoid being severely penalized later. The easiest method is to be very candid with the other directors and to have their acknowledgment recorded in the minutes of the meeting.

Should disclosure have to be made to the shareholders, very often they are the other directors and, if they approve the contract by special resolution, it will cost some minority shareholder a lot of money to go to court to have the contract set aside on the grounds that it was not fair and reasonable at the time it was made.

Finally, even if the interest of a director or officer in a contract is never disclosed, the contract is still valid until the court sets it aside, or stops its completion on the application of a shareholder or "some interested party." The company itself cannot avoid the contract at its own option.

You should bear in mind, however, that directors who have failed to disclose a personal interest or profit in a contract entered into by the company have been treated very severely by the courts and have lost far more than the profit in the long run.

3. Personal liability (section 151)

If you contravene the provisions of the Company Act and if the company is proven to have suffered damages as a result of your contravention, you will be *personally liable* to make up those damages. You are bound by these provisions even if you live outside the province.

However, you will not be held accountable under this section if you prove that you did not know and could not reasonably have known that the act authorized by the resolution contravened the Company Act. You are also entitled to rely and act in good faith upon the financial statements of the company that are presented to you by its officers. If a resolution was passed approving something that contravenes the act and you dissented and had your dissent recorded in writing, you will also have a strong defence.

Furthermore, even if you knowingly breached this section, there is a two-year limitation period imposed on any action brought under this section. This may effectively prevent liquidators, trustees in bankruptcy, and shareholders from taking any action.

As a director you should also be aware of the Payment of Wages Act which makes all directors and officers personally liable for the unpaid wages of an employee up to a maximum of two months' wages for each employee who has not been paid.

4. Liability under the Income Tax Act

If your corporation fails to deduct and remit income tax from employees' salaries, the directors and the corporation will be jointly liable for the amount that should have been paid, plus interest and penalties. Any director who has shown a degree of care to prevent the non-payment and remittance of the income tax may not be liable.

If any action is to be taken against a director on this point, it must be commenced no later than two years after he or she ceased to be a director.

g. YOUR ESCAPE ROUTES

Suppose you do breach one of the provisions of the act, and are therefore accountable to the company or to the shareholders under the insider trading provision. Or, suppose you are guilty of an offence under the act and are subject to a fine. What can you do?

(a) You may obtain shareholder approval for the violation that will absolve you of a breach of your common-law or equitable duties (i.e., to act as a reasonable, prudent person in good faith).

(b) The court may approve and allow the company to indemnify you against any liability you incur, even if it is the company itself that brings the action against you. To take advantage of this provision, you must prove that you were acting in good faith, honestly, and reasonably. The court must also feel that you should honestly and reasonably be excused.

(c) You as a director can protect yourself by purchasing liability insurance, without shareholder approval! However, this does not cover officers, only directors; arguably, it covers only the liability incurred under section 151. This insurance is not cheap and, in the case of a small non-reporting company involved in a speculative venture, it would be prohibitively expensive.

13
SHAREHOLDER RIGHTS AND REMEDIES

The act gives quite broad rights to shareholders and they can be broken down into the following categories.

(a) The "oppression" remedy may be invoked when the conduct of the majority of shareholders is oppressive or unfairly prejudicial to the minority (section 224).

(b) A "derivative" action may be brought by a shareholder on behalf of a company when the company, for some reason, will not initiate the action (section 225).

(c) The "dissent" remedy may be invoked by a shareholder who has the right to dissent and require the company to purchase his or her shares (section 231).

(d) There are situations where a shareholder can apply for a winding-up of the company (section 295).

a. WHAT IS OPPRESSIVE OR PREJUDICIAL CONDUCT? (section 224)

You should note that the oppression section is directed to wrongs done to the *member* and not wrongs done to the company.

Before section 224 was passed, an applicant for a winding-up order had to show that there were grounds to wind up the company. This is no longer required, nor is it necessary for the applicant to prove that the affairs of the company are "oppressive to some part of the members" including the applicant.

Section 224 simply provides that if the affairs of the company or the powers of the directors are being exercised in an oppressive manner, *or* that some act of the company has been done or is threatened, *or* some resolution of the members or any class of members has been passed or is proposed that is unfairly prejudicial, then an application for a winding-up order may be brought.

The act attempts to broaden the court's traditionally narrow view of oppressive conduct by referring to conduct that is "unfairly prejudicial." In any event, conduct that is oppressive or unfairly prejudicial can be determined only by the facts in each case.

For example, if you could show that you were the victim of "share watering" (as when newly issued shares are not offered to shareholders on a pro rata basis), or that you had suffered damages as a minority shareholder because of a breach of the act, you may have rights under the oppression remedy. Your relief as a minority shareholder is set out in section 224.

b. REPRESENTATIVE ACTIONS ON BEHALF OF THE COMPANY (section 225)

As in the previous section, the concern here is the right of a minority (i.e., those controlling less than 50% of the voting shares).

Minority shareholders suits are an attempt to force the directors (usually the majority shareholders) to do something for the benefit of, or stop doing something that is harmful to, the company and the minority shareholders.

Since it is the company that is supposed to be suffering, in normal circumstances it would be the company that would take the action. However, the minority, not being in control of the board of directors, cannot get the company to act. Consequently, they can sue only as representatives of the company and the result is that the money recovered in a successful suit belongs to the company and not to the individual minority shareholders who took the action. You should note the practice that gives the minority costs of the action, if they win.

Past cases indicate that a minority is entitled to sue in a representative way in the following situations:

(a) When the company is doing or intends to do something beyond its powers. (This would only be applicable to British Columbia companies with restricted objects in the memorandum.)

(b) When the company is doing or intends to do something which constitutes a fraud on the minority and the persons controlling the company's activities are the beneficiaries of the fraud.

(c) When a resolution has been or is proposed to be passed which requires more than 50% of the voting shares but is or has been passed by only 50% of the voting shares.

(d) In any other case where the interests of justice require that the rule be disregarded.

You often hear this type of proceeding referred to as a "class," "representative," or "derivative" action.

If you are a director, you may use these proceedings even if you do not own one share of the company — but, practically speaking, problems arise when one or more persons initiate and carry forward a representative action. These problems have been considered in the act and the following provisions have been made.

One person may be appointed by the court to conduct the action on behalf of all those who are complaining. Section 225 is an attempt to control the problems experienced by the people who actively carry on the litigation, as their rights to settle the action before and after trial are not very clear and, all too often, they receive very little support from the other shareholders whom they claim to represent.

Costs may also be recovered during and after the course of the action which helps with the financing of such a suit.

c. DISSENT PROCEEDINGS BY SHAREHOLDERS (section 231)

This particular remedy is probably the most effective for most shareholders. In short, it provides that, in certain situations where a minority shareholder dissents to a proceeding by the company, the company must purchase his or her shares at fair market value. The parties must agree on fair market value and, if there is no agreement, they can apply to the court for a determination of the question.

Dissent proceedings may be taken under section 231 in certain circumstances, provided that the member has given the directors the necessary notice within the time prescribed by the act.

Every time a company proposes to pass a special resolution, you, as a director, should automatically consider whether the dissent proceedings of the act may be brought into play.

This section may be used for purposes that were not intended because many shareholders will be tempted to become creditors (i.e., the company must purchase the shares). How far the courts will go in preventing this remains to be seen.

What happens under this section, once the shares have been purchased, is a reduction of the capital of the company. All that is necessary under section 231(4)(b) is for the court "to have due regard for the rights of creditors." It is not necessary for real creditors to consent to the reduction of capital.

d. INVOLUNTARY WINDING-UP (section 295)

Under the act, the court can order the winding-up of the company when a member, creditor, or other interested party applies for it if the court thinks it just and equitable. Because of the division of legislative responsibility in Canada, an insolvent company in British Columbia must be put into bankruptcy or wound up under the provision of the federal Winding-up Act.

Therefore, winding-up under the "just and equitable" rule in British Columbia will take place for reasons like "justifiable lack of confidence in the conduct of the company's affairs," "misapplication of the company's property," or "deadlock in the management of the company."

In addition, if the memorandum and articles provide for the winding-up on the happening of an event, the court may make an order under this section on application by the appropriate person.

This provision allows for the speedy winding-up of a company under the articles instead of litigation between the shareholders as to whether or not the company should be wound up.

14

HOW TO CHANGE YOUR COMPANY NAME
OR CHANGE OFFICES

a. CHANGING THE COMPANY NAME

So you've been operating a couple of years and you've come to the realization that the name "Slipshod Industries Ltd." was not the most brilliant of ideas.

Or perhaps the name no longer reflects what you do. Perhaps it has caused you unforeseen problems, such as midnight telephone calls at your home by stranded motorists who are able to trace you through a name like "Marvin Mechanic Towing Services." Or perhaps "North End Appliance Repairs" is now embarrassing because you have moved to the south end of town.

Whatever the reason, it is possible to change your company name by a simple procedure. You must go through the same reservation procedure and pay the name search and reservation fee as discussed in chapter 4. A special resolution to change the company name can be consented to in writing and signed by all the members (see Sample #35) and the altered memorandum prepared and attached (see Sample #36). After obtaining all members' signatures on the special resolution and filing it in the minute book under members' minutes and resolutions, you are ready to prepare a certified copy of the resolution on form 21 to send to the Registrar of Companies (see Sample #37). You should send two copies of the form 21 with the attached memorandum so you will receive a stamped copy back for your minute book along with the new certificate. A covering letter is shown as Sample #38. A cheque covering the fees* and made payable to the Minister of Finance should accompany these documents.

If your company deals in land or intends to purchase property under the new company name, you will need to check the *British Columbia Gazette* about a month after you receive the change of name certificate to obtain the *Gazette* reference.

One final comment about changing a company name: if you want a catchy name primarily for advertising value, it may not be necessary for you to go through this process. You can simply adopt a trade name with no forms to fill out as long as your intention is not to steal someone else's name or defraud your creditors in any way.

So, for example, J & J Industries Ltd. may be operating the "Pipe and Pot Shop." Your letterhead and signs, etc., would then have to read:

JJ's PIPE AND POT SHOP
owned and operated by
J & J Industries Ltd.

or

JJ's PIPE AND POT SHOP
(a division of)
J & J Industries Ltd.

---

*Current fees for changing the name of your company may be obtained by contacting the Registrar of Companies at 387-7848. Fees at the time of publication were: name change — $100; name approval fee — $30; certification — $25.

SPECIAL RESOLUTION TO CHANGE COMPANY NAME

J & J INDUSTRIES LTD.
(the "Company")

We, the undersigned, being all the members of the company, hereby consent in writing to the following special resolutions:

RESOLVED that:

1.   Pursuant to section 241 of the Company Act, the name of the company be changed from J & J INDUSTRIES LTD. to JJ's PIPE AND POT SHOP LTD. and that the memorandum be amended accordingly.
2.   The altered memorandum be attached as Schedule "A."

DATED as of the 6th day of July, 199-.

_____
JOHN DOE

_____
JACK DOE

SAMPLE #36
ALTERED MEMORANDUM

SCHEDULE "A"

Form 1
(Section 5)

COMPANY ACT

ALTERED MEMORANDUM

(as altered by resolution passed July 6, 199-)

1.   The name of the company is JJ's PIPE AND POT SHOP LTD.

2.   The authorized capital of the company consists of TEN THOUSAND (10 000) Common shares without par value.

(If you use "a division of," those three words must be in parentheses.) In this way you avoid any problems of being accused of misleading customers or creditors. It's all perfectly legal and may be a simpler method of getting what you want.

b. CHANGING YOUR RECORDS OR REGISTERED OFFICE

If you are keeping your own records and you move, you must inform the Registrar of Companies by preparing documents according to the following procedure.

Prepare a directors' consent resolution, in writing, as shown in Sample #39. After obtaining all directors' signatures on this resolution, prepare a Notice to Change Office (see Sample #40), and file it in duplicate with the Registrar of Companies along with the filing fee. The change does not become effective until two copies of the notice have been filed with the Registrar.

If you decide to use a law firm as your company's registered and records office address, they will prepare the appropriate documents.

Ministry of Finance and Corporate Relations
REGISTRAR OF COMPANIES
Corporate, Central and Mobile Home Registry
940 Blanshard Street
Victoria, B.C. V8W 3E6

SPECIAL RESOLUTION
Form 21
(Section 371)

COMPANY ACT

Certificate of Incorporation No. _123456_

The following special* resolution was passed by the undermentioned company on the date stated:

Name of company: _J & J Industries Ltd._

Date resolution passed: _July 6, 199-_

Resolution:

RESOLVED THAT:

1. Pursuant to Section 241 of the Company Act, the name of the company be changed from J & J INDUSTRIES LTD. to JJ'S PIPE AND POT SHOP LTD. and that the memorandum be amended accordingly.

2. The altered memorandum be attached as Schedule "A".

Certified a true copy the _____ day of _____ , 19 _____ .

John Doe
_____
(signature)

_____
Director
(relationship to company)

NOTE: - FILING FEE: $15.00
     - A $5.00 re-examination fee shall apply on documents which have been rejected owing to an error or omission.
    * See section 1(1) for definition of "special resolution."

Ministry of Finance and Corporate Relations
Corporate, Central and Mobile Home Registry
940 Blanshard Street
Victoria, B.C.
V8W 3E6

July 7, 199-

Dear Registrar:

Re: J & J INDUSTRIES LTD. #123456

Enclosed please find the following:

1. Duplicate copies of the Special Resolution to Change the Company's Name

2. Duplicate copies of altered Memorandum (Schedule "A")

3. Certified cheque payable to the Minister of Finance for the sum of $110.

We have reserved the name JJ's Pipe and Pot Shop Ltd. under number 63574. Would you kindly process the change of name application and forward to me the change of name certificate.

Thank you for your cooperation.

Yours truly,

John Doe

John Doe

J & J INDUSTRIES LTD.
(the "Company")

Pursuant to the Company Act the following resolutions are passed by the directors of the company, consented to in writing by all the directors of the company:

RESOLVED that the registered and records offices of the company be changed from 123 West First Street, Somewhere, B.C. V7J 1H1 to #201 - 600 Main Street, Nowhere, B.C. V1P 0G0.

DATED as of the 15th day of August, 199-.

_____
JOHN DOE

_____
JACK DOE

NOTICE TO CHANGE OFFICES

PROVINCE OF BRITISH COLUMBIA

FORM 4
(Section 40)

Certificate of Incorporation No. ___123 456___

COMPANY ACT

NOTICE TO CHANGE OFFICE

The location of the following office(s) of the undermentioned company has been changed as follows:

Name of company ___J & J Industries Ltd.___

REGISTERED OFFICE*

From

Former address ___123 West First Street___
         Somewhere ZIP 0G0

_____, B.C.

To

New address ___600 Main Street___
         Nowhere ZIP 0G0

_____, B.C.

RECORDS OFFICE*

From

Former address ___123 West First Street___
         Somewhere ZIP 0G0

_____, B.C.

To

New address ___600 Main Street___
         Nowhere ZIP 0G0

_____, B.C.

Dated the ___20th___day of ___August___, 19_9_.

(Signature) _____

___Director_____
(Relationship to company)

* The address of each office must be adequate to enable a person readily to find the office.
NOTE — This form is to be sent in duplicate to the Registrar of Companies, Victoria, B.C.

129

15
HOW TO DISSOLVE YOUR COMPANY

Eventually, you may decide that it is no longer worthwhile for you to continue doing business as a company because, for example, the directors wish to retire, or substantially all of the assets and inventory of the company have been sold. In this situation you are entitled to rely on the procedure set out in section 282, which is tailor-made for small non-reporting companies.

Although it appears from the wording of the section that there have to be at least two directors to sign the statutory declaration, if yours is a one-person company, you are still entitled to use this dissolution process. If there are more than two directors, only two of them need sign the statutory declaration form.

First, bring your company up to date with the Registrar by making up all unfiled annual reports, then pay off the creditors of the company or else receive written waivers of their claims. Don't forget that if you made a loan to the company or transferred assets to it in exchange for a promissory note, you are personally entitled to be a creditor of the company and receive repayment of this debt.

As a shareholder, you are also entitled to share in any of the assets or money remaining after discharging all debts, on the basis of the number of issued shares you hold in the company.

Second, the shareholders must pass an ordinary resolution, either at a specially called meeting or in writing, requesting the Registrar to strike the company off the register (see Sample #41).

Then take a form 20 and copy the information from the ordinary resolution as signed by all the members onto the form 20 and have it signed and dated by a director (see Sample #42). This will be the copy that you send to the Registrar of Companies.

The third step in the process is for two directors to make out a statutory declaration in which they state how the assets have been distributed and that there are no debts or liabilities owing by the company (see Sample #43 for a guide).

You may alter the body of the declaration to fit your particular circumstances, but keep the opening and closing clauses similar to the example.

You will then take your resolution, a copy of it, and the statutory declaration form to a notary who will swear out the statutory declaration for you, and certify the copy of your resolution as a true copy. This should cost about $25 if you have already drawn up the forms.

Mail your statutory declaration and the certified copy of the resolution to the Registrar of Companies together with a cheque to cover the filing fees*. If the shareholders resolved to surrender the Certificate of Incorporation, as in the first of the sample resolutions, you must send along your Certificate of Incorporation as well. You should also send a letter like the one in Sample #44 with your forms to make sure that no confusion arises.

---

*For current fees, contact the Registrar of Companies at 387-7848. At the time of publication, the fee for filing documents associated with dissolution of a company was $40.

If all your forms are in order, the Registrar will then publish in the *Gazette* a notice of the company being struck off the register. You may note the volume and page number of this notice for future references by looking it up in your local library or by purchasing a copy of the notice concerning your company from Crown Publications, just as you did for your incorporation notice (see chapter 4, section **g.**). Refer to the confirming memorandum that you received from the Registrar to find the date on which the company was ordered struck off the register.

Remember that a company may be struck off the register if it fails to file annual reports for two consecutive years. If you let your company die this slow death, valuable assets may be left in the name of the company, and it is very difficult to transfer them to a creditor or purchaser without going through an expensive reinstatement process.

If you do not do this, the assets escheat (are forfeited to) the Crown in the right of the province. Rarely does the Crown ever take possession of such an asset as it usually waits for years before taking any action upon this right. However, it is most inconvenient to suddenly, for example, decide you want to sell that piece of land registered in the name of your holding company when the company has been struck off the register. For this reason it is best to properly dissolve your company by resolution and disperse the assets so that there are no loose ends that can come back to haunt you.

J & J INDUSTRIES LTD.
(the "Company")

We, the undersigned, being all the members of the company, hereby consent in writing to the following resolutions:

RESOLVED that:

1. The Registrar of Companies for the Province of British Columbia be requested to strike the company off the Register.
2. As incidental to the foregoing, the property of J & J INDUSTRIES LTD., if any, be distributed rateably among the members of the company according to their rights and interest in the company.

OR

WHEREAS:

A. The company has sold all of its assets to John Doe, 111A Street, Anywhere, B.C. in consideration for the reduction of the amount owing by the company to the said John Doe.
B. The company does not carry on any business, and
C. The company has no liabilities to any creditors, except $400 due and owing to Heather Doe of 444D Street, Anywhere, B.C. which amount Heather Doe has agreed to forgive and forget.

RESOLVED that:

1. The Certificate of Incorporation of the company be surrendered to the Registrar of Companies for the province of British Columbia and the said Registrar be requested to strike the company off the Registrar.

Note: If you use this clause you will have to submit your Certificate of Incorporation.

DATED this 9th day of July, 199-.

JOHN DOE   JACK DOE

                                            JEAN DOE

132

FORM 20

(Section 371)

PROVINCE OF BRITISH COLUMBIA

———

Certificate of
Incorporation No. _123456_

COMPANY ACT

———

ORDINARY RESOLUTION

The following ordinary resolution was passed by the undermentioned Company on the date stated:

Name of Company: _____ J & J INDUSTRIES LTD. _____

_____

Date resolution passed: _____ June 15 _____ , 19 9- .

Resolution:

RESOLVED that:

1. The Registrar of Companies for the Province of British Columbia be requested to strike the Company off the Register.

2. As incidental to the foregoing, the property of J & J INDUSTRIES LTD., if any, be distributed rateably among the Members of the Company according to their rights and interests in the Company."

Certifed a true copy this _____ day of _____ , 19 ____ .

(Signature) _____ John Doe. _____

(Relationship to Company) _____ (Director or Officer) _____

STATUTORY DECLARATION

WE, JOHN DOE of 111A Street, in the City of Anywhere, in the Province of British Columbia, Businessman, and JACK DOE of 222B Street, in the City of Anywhere, in the Province of British Columbia, Businessman, do so severally and solemnly declare that:

1. I, the said John Doe for myself declare that I have been a director of J & J Industries Ltd., since the 25th day of July, 1990 and have personal knowledge of the matters herein declared by me.

2. I, the said Jack Doe for myself declare that I have been a director of J & J Industries Ltd., since the 1st day of July, 1990 and have personal knowledge of the matters herein declared by me.

3. J & J Industries has parted with its assets by distributing the same rateably among its shareholders according to their rights and interest in the company.

4. That J & J Industries Ltd., has no debts and liabilities.

AND WE SEVERALLY make this solemn declaration conscientiously believing it to be true and knowing that it is of the same force and effect as if made under oath and by virtue of the Canada Evidence Act.

SEVERALLY DECLARED before me each of the above named deponents at the City of Anywhere in the Province of British Columbia, this 6th day of December, 199-.

John Doe
_____
JOHN DOE

Jack Doe
_____
JACK DOE

J.M. Commissioner
_____
A Commissioner for taking Affidavits within the
Province of British Columbia

John Doe,
111 A Street
Anywhere, B.C. V1P 0G0

December 6, 199-

Ministry of Finance and Corporate Relations
Corporate, Central and Mobile Home Registry
940 Blanshard Street,
Victoria, B.C.
V8W 3E6

Dear Registrar:

Re: <u>Dissolution of J & J Industries Ltd. #123456</u>

Enclosed herewith are the following documents:

1.   Certified copy of the Ordinary Resolution requesting you to strike the said company off the register.

2.   Statutory declaration of John Doe and Jack Doe, directors of the company.

3.   Certificate of Incorporation No. 123456

Would you kindly attend to the striking off of the said company and mail the confirming memorandum to the above address.

Yours truly,

John Doe

John Doe

APPENDIX
CHECKLIST OF STEPS TO BE FOLLOWED

✓   Name decided on

✓   Letter to Companies Office in Victoria reserving name along with cheque to cover name reservation fee, or file Name Approval Request form along with fee at your local B.C. Access Centre

✓   Incorporation service requested or package forms ordered

✓   Memorandum prepared

_____   Articles prepared

✓   Notice of Offices prepared

✓   Documents forwarded to Registrar:

    (i)   Original and copy of memorandum and articles

    (ii)   Original and copy of Notice of Offices

    (iii)   Cheque payable to Minister of Finance for incorporation fees

✓   Incorporation documents received back from Victoria

_____   Minute book purchased

_____   Seal ordered

✓   Banking resolutions completed, and account opened

_____   Minutes or consent resolutions of various meetings drawn and signed:

    (i)   Resolutions of Subscribers to Memorandum

    (ii)   Resolutions of Directors

_____   Notice of Directors filed (if applicable)

_____   Share certificates issued

_____   Minute book opened and originals of minutes and copies of all other documents inserted in chronological order

_____   Miscellaneous steps:

    (i)   Assets transferred to company by drafting minutes, etc.

    (ii)   Social Services Tax Department visited for exemption form

    (iii)   If motor vehicle(s) involved, Motor Vehicle Branch visited for transfer purposes

_____   Annual Report filed

OTHER TITLES IN THE
SELF-COUNSEL BUSINESS SERIES

FORMING AND MANAGING A NON-PROFIT ORGANIZATION IN CANADA

by Flora MacLeod

$19.95

Maybe there's an issue in your community you feel strongly about, or you'd like to start a neighborhood action group to deal with a local problem, or revitalize and re-organize an existing group. What's the next step?

This book takes you through the first steps of finding like-minded people, writing a goal statement, and choosing a name for your group, as well as outlining basic organizational structures. The book tells you how to run your organization and maintain good records, as well as how to write funding proposals, how to fulfill yearly form filing requirements, and when to hire staff.

Samples of all the forms you will need to become registered as a non-profit organization are included on a province-by-province basis.

Some of the topics included are —

- Why you need a board of directors
- Why maintaining good records will help you write funding proposals
- Writing your constitution
- Strategies for gaining support for your organization
- The GST rebate available to registered non-profit organizations
- Future trends for non-profit organizations

BASIC ACCOUNTING FOR THE SMALL BUSINESS

Simple, foolproof techniques for keeping your books straight and staying out of trouble

by Clive Cornish, C.G.A.

$8.95

Having bookkeeping problems? Do you feel you should know more about book-keeping, but simply don't have time for a course? Do you wish that the paperwork in your business could be improved, but you don't know where or how to start?

This book is a down-to-earth manual on how to save your accountant's time and your time and money. Written in clear, everyday English, not in accounting jargon, this guide will help you and your office staff keep better records.

Inside you will find illustrations of sample forms and instructions on how to prepare all the records you will need to keep, including:

- Daily cash sheet
- Cash summary
- Statement ledger
- Payables journal
- Synoptic journal
- Payroll book
- Income statement
- Trial balance
- Columnar work sheet

LOOK BEFORE YOU LEAP: MARKET RESEARCH MADE EASY

by Don Doman, Dell Dennison, and Margaret Doman

$14.95

Market research is vital if you want to stay in touch with your customers and your industry. Whether you are starting a new business, launching a product, setting a marketable price point, or simply trying to increase your market share, market research can tell you what you need to know. A successful business can't do without it.

The good news is that you *can* do it yourself. Market research is not the exclusive province of high-priced professionals. It is simply a process of asking questions or finding existing information about the market, your competition, and potential customers.

This practical, easy-to-read book will lead you through the process of planning, implementing, and analyzing market research for your company. It answers questions such as:

- When should I do market research?
- Where can I find the data I need?
- Who are my best survey subjects?
- How do I design a market research questionnaire?
- Why should I use brainstorming sessions and focus groups in my research?
- Where can I rent a mailing list?
- When do I need to hire a professional?
- How do I analyze the data I find?

With this guide in hand, you can easily carry out the market research you need to point you toward successful ventures and avoid disastrous ones.

ORDER FORM

All prices are subject to change without notice. Books are available in book, department, and stationery stores. If you cannot buy the book through a store, please use this order form. (Please print.)

Name _____

Address _____

_____

Charge to: ❑ Visa   ❑ MasterCard

Account Number _____

Validation Date_____

Expiry Date _____

Signature _____

YES, please send me:

_____**Forming and Managing
 a Non-Profit Organization** $19.95

_____**Basic Accounting** $ 8.95

_____**Look Before You Leap:
 Market Research Made Easy** $14.95

Please add $3.00 for postage & handling. Canadian residents, please add 7% GST to your order. WA residents, please add 7.8% sales tax.

❑ **Check here for a free catalogue.**

Please send your order to:
  Self-Counsel Press
  1481 Charlotte Road
  North Vancouver, B.C. V7J 1H1

Visit our Internet Web Site at:
http://www.self-counsel.com/